The Easy

Tree
Guide

The Easy
Tree
Guide

Common Native and
Cultivated Trees of
the United States
and Canada

Keith Rushforth

Paintings by Gill Tomblin
and Ann Winterbotham

FALCON®

GUILFORD, CONNECTICUT
HELENA, MONTANA
AN IMPRINT OF THE GLOBE PEQUOT PRESS

Published by
The Globe Pequot Press, Inc., P.O. Box 480, Guilford, Connecticut 06437, www.GlobePequot.com
Falcon and FalconGuide are registered trademarks of The Globe Pequot Press.

Library of Congress Cataloging-in-Publication Data is available.
ISBN 0-7627-3068-4

Tree heights given in this guide are given to the nearest foot, but of course variations should be expected.

Conceived, edited, designed and produced by
Duncan Petersen Publishing, 31, Ceylon Road, London W14 OPY

Editorial Director Andrew Duncan
Art Editor Keith Davis
Editor Sophie Page
Text by Keith Rushforth
Consultant Dr. Glenn D. Dreyer
Paintings by Gill Tomblin and Ann Winterbotham

Photographs by
Frank Lane Picture Agency, GardenWorld, Dr. Glenn D. Dreyer, Dr. Michael Dirr, Alexander Duncan, Larissa Haney, Robin Orans/Gardenscape, Martin Jukes/Alice Holt Lodge, Keith Rushforth

Printed in Portugal by Printer Portuguesa

Contents

About This Book

CAN A TREE GUIDE *REALLY* BE EASY?

Yes: trees are readily identified – with the right information at hand – because they can be examined at leisure. It's also helpful that they provide identification features ('characters') throughout the year. While it is true that trees are easier to identify at some times than others, if needs must, you can tell tree from tree at any season.

Perhaps the main problem people have with tree identification is the variability of trees; and that sometimes (especially in woodland), the leaves are out of reach.

HOW EASY?

In making this *the* Easy Tree Guide, we have concentrated on several key points:

■ **The photographs are, for a tree field guide, uniquely large and clear,** and designed to work hand in hand with the **paintings** (the artwork). For maximum ease of comparison, they face each other on opposite pages of each double page spread in the guide.

Photographs can't be equalled for an overall impression of a tree, while the artwork panel highlights the details essential for identification and allows comparison with other species. You'll find it valuable to let your eyes roam between the two, associating details in the artwork panel with the whole tree.

Typical barks are shown in separate small photographs, another very useful feature.

■ **Simple language** The text is an easy read for anyone, avoiding jargon and technical terms. The captions in the artwork panel highlight the key identification features of the paintings.

■ **Important variations** are described in the captions to the artwork and the photographs.

■ **The distribution** and **preferred habitat** of each species are described in the main text under the artwork panel.

THE APPEAL OF TREES

Trees stir the emotions, whether we want to embrace them or chop them down. They are large, and can appear to live forever. They make landmarks and meeting places; they give character to our towns; and they play a major role in defining our landscapes. They cause problems, such as shading houses and cutting out sunlight; they drop debris; and they harbor pests such as squirrels and birds. They are useful, not just for timber and firewood, but because they shade our houses, brighten our gardens with their flowers and fruits, and provide homes for many a creature, including squirrels and pigeons. Genesis chapter 2, verse 9, sums it up in simplistic, but timeless, Biblical style: trees are *'pleasing to the eye and good for food'*. At times we may love them or hate them, but we can't ignore them.

There are about 700 trees native to North America plus many cultivated or naturalized ones, including 90 oaks and half as many pines, which alone are enough to fill the entire book. The guide features the commonest trees both in forests and in parks and gardens, and some of the most interesting trees. If you need a guide that covers every single tree, see the suggestions on page 288.

Technical Terms

In this guide, technical terms are accompanied by a simple definition in (we hope) plain English. This glossary offers a somewhat fuller explanation of terms used, as well as covering some additional botanical terms in common use.

alternate: leaves or buds that emerge first on one side of a twig, then the other.

annual shoot: the growth made in a single year.

aril: fleshy or juicy base to a fruit, see yew (pages 44–45).

auriculate: with ear-like lobes.

bastard: hybrid between two species.

bole: trunk of a tree.

bract: structure (derived from a leaf) beneath a flower or fruit. It can be leafy, but not necessarily.

capsule: a dry fruit with two or more cells, and which opens when ripe.

catkin: male or female flower without petals – often their pollen spreads on the wind. Usually hangs down.

cluster: where several parts occur together.

crown: upper part of a tree which has the leaves.

decussate: leaves in opposite pairs, with the alternate pairs at right angles to the pair above and below.

digitate: with finger-like leaflets from a common point.

dioecious: with male and female flowers on separate trees.

drupe: fruit in which the seed is protected by a stony layer, outside which is a fleshy covering (eg, a cherry).

fascicle (of needles): bundle of needles.

foliage: leaves and twigs.

habit: overall form or growth pattern.

heterosis: extra vigor shown by a hybrid.

lamina: blade or flat part of leaf.

lanceolate: lance shaped.

leaflets: separate divisions of a compound leaf.

leaf veins: veins in leaf which transport water and nutrients.

linear (of leaves): a narrow, straight leaf.

lobe: projection on leaf margin—may be round or pointed.

long shoot: extension or lengthening shoot, and only significant on trees which have short shoots; for example, larch and cedars.

needle: leaf of a conifer, often but not always sharp.

net-veined: when the veins form a visible network on a leaf.

obovate: egg shaped but broadest above the middle.

opposite: buds or leaves arranged in pairs on twig.

ovate: egg shaped but broadest below the middle.

palmate: with veins or leaflets starting from the end of the leaf stalk.

panicle: a branched, compound flower head (inflorescence) with many individual flowers.

paripinnate: pinnate, with an even number of pairs of leaflets.

petiole: leaf stalk.

pinnate: compound leaf where the leaflets arise successively from a central stalk.

pioneer species: the first to grow in (colonize) a bare site.

pod: fruit of a legume, such as a pea.

phyllode: a shoot modified to act as a leaf.

radial: like bicycle spokes.

scale leaf: small leaf of some conifers, see cypress family.

shoot: extension growth.

short shoot: which lengthens a little each year.

stamen: male parts of a flower, with an anther or pollen-producing part at the tip.

stipule: growth similar to leaf, but not a leaf, at base of leaf stalk.

style: female part of a flower, with pollen-receiving **stigma** at the tip.

sucker: shoot growing directly from a root or base of trunk.

symbiosis: when two dissimilar organisms live together.

toothed: small, irregular points on leaf margin.

unisexual: of a single sex (most flowers contain both male and female parts).

verticillate: in whorls. A whorl is a number of parts occuring together at more or less the same points.

An Introduction to Trees

WHAT IS A TREE?

This apparently simple question is surprisingly difficult to answer precisely. A tree must have a woody stem, but so must a shrub. The defining factor, then, must be ability to grow to a large size. But how large is 'large'? In this guide, our watershed is 16 ½ ft; below that, it's generally safe to consider it a shrub. Most of the trees featured in this guide can grow to 50 ft or more, and some will grow to 200 ft in a favorable place; but a few common trees, such as rowan, are usually around 35 ft when fully grown.

NAMING TREES

All trees have several names, and these fall into two main categories: common names and scientific (or Latin) names. Common names are extremely variable, and frequently confusing. Rowan is often called mountain ash, but has nothing to do with the true ashes (apart from the superficial similarity of the leaves), and grows in lowland woodland as well as up on mountains. Eastern red-cedar (*Juniperus virginiana*) is in a different genus from Western red-cedar (*Thuja plicata*), and along with incense-cedar (*Calocedrus decurrens*) is in a different family from the true cedars (*Cedrus*).

Botany uses a unique Latin name for each species, recognized the world over. It consists of two parts: the first part, the genus, describes its immediate group: *Sorbus* and *Acer* are both genus names. The second part is the specific name, such as *aucuparia* for rowan and *negundo* for box elder. This pins it down to one particular species. In botany, there can be only a single genus with the same name and in each genus there can be only one species with any one specific name. However, the same specific name can be used in another genus. The specific name often tells you something about the plant: for instance pungens in both *Pinus pungens* and *Picea pungens* tells you that they have sharp points—to the cones in the pine (*Pinus*) and to the needles in the spruce (*Picea*).

Despite Latin names being unique, a tree may get two or more of them. However, the oldest validly published name has precedence, and the newer names rank as synonyms. Some common synonyms are given in the index.

Although not important in an easy tree guide, botany ranks all species in a hierarchy. Individual species are essentially the lowest 'rank' – though subspecies, varieties or forms are one lower. Next up from species are the genera (plural of genus*);* genera are placed in families (for instance, willows and poplars are in the *Salicaceae* or willow family); and families are placed in orders. The conifers in this guide belong to several families (*Araucariaceae, Cupressaceae, Pinaceae* and *Taxodiaceae*), but all belong to one order, *Coniferales*, except for the yews or *Taxus*, which are always placed in their own family, *Taxaceae,* and often in their own order, the *Taxales*. Likewise gingko or maidenhair tree, which has its own family, *Ginkgoaceae,* and order, *Ginkgoales*.

Next up in the hierarchy, above order, comes 'class'. There are two classes: *Gymnospermae*, literally 'naked seeds'; and *Angiospermae*, literally 'hidden seeds'. This last is divided into two subclasses, *Dicotyledoneae* (having two seed leaves and secondary thickening of stems) and the *Monocotyledoneae* (having one seed leaf and lacking the capacity to make secondary thickening). *Dicotyledoneae* (frequently shortened to Dicots) include all the broadleaved trees; and *Monocotyledoneae* (shortened to Monocots) include the palms (also grasses and orchids) whose leaves have parallel veins. Both contain many orders and families.

FINDING A TREE – THROUGH THE INDEX

Any tree in the guide can of course be reached via the index, pages 284-288, listing both scientific and common names. As you become more familiar with trees, you will use the index increasingly. But, however efficient an index may be, it is useless if you don't know the tree's name in the first place.

FINDING A TREE – IF YOU DON'T KNOW ITS NAME

If you're starting from scratch – typically with a twig and some leaves gathered on a walk – simply browse through the book, comparing what you have with the artwork and photographs. With more than 270 pages to get through, this might seem a daunting task; but it's not as difficult as you might think.

The order in which the species fall is designed to help. The book groups them according to leaf shape. The book

Western red-cedar

starts with ginkgo (pages 14-15) and monkey puzzle (pages 16-17): special cases which are best got out of the way first. Then the remainder of the conifers follow in a logical order: those with small scale-like leaves come first (pages 18-35); then trees with 'needle' leaves (pages 36-81); and finally the pines

Above, deodar cedar: needle leaves.

(pages 70-97), with needle leaves in bundles of two to five.

The broadleaved section (pages 102-237 and 282-283) starts with trees that have simple leaves. In this section, related trees are generally placed together, but leaves with small lobes come first, followed by those with large lobes; however, alder and birch, with toothed (not lobed) leaves, come

Pinus taeda

Introductions to conifers and broadleaves, pages 12-13 and 98-101

These two spreads can speed up the process of getting to roughly the right page of the guide. They are a visual key, breaking down the contents into groups whose foliage looks roughly similar.

right at the beginning and the trees with more strongly lobed leaves, such as sycamore, at the end. Even this order is not absolute: for instance, white poplar (pages 126-127) is placed with the other poplars, despite its strongly lobed leaves.

American aspen

The broadleaved trees with compound, pinnate leaves (divided into leaflets) are on pages 238-269, with horse chestnuts (leaves compound, but like a palm's) as a one-off on pages 270-273. The palms, with their immense compound leaves, are on pages 274-281.

Sycamore maple: strongly lobed.

The main text descriptions

These generally start with information on the tree's native range – those parts of the world (often far from North America) where it grows naturally. The rest of the text deals with the tree as Americans will find it. To avoid repetition, the fact that trees have been much transported into America from around the world and naturalized here is taken as understood.

Features That Identify Trees

This guide uses obvious identification features or characters rather than detailed botanical ones. (This explains some of the ordering, such as box elder (*Acer negundo*) being placed with the pinnate-leaved trees (pages 252-253) and several pages after the other maples. Trees, like other higher plants ('higher' as opposed to the 'lower' plants, such as ferns, mosses), have stems with bark, shoots, buds, leaves, flowers and fruits, and these are the characteristics which the guide describes.

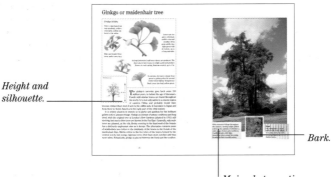

Height and silhouette.

Bark.

Main photo caption.

Height and silhouette The height range of an average mature tree is given in the small panel on the left-hand page of each spread, below the main artwork panel. Here you will also see a silhouette of the tree, emphasizing its typical outline. For evergreen trees (most conifers and some broadleaves), the silhouettes are of course the same all year; for deciduous trees, the winter silhouette, without foliage, is given.

Bark This can be very informative and diagnostic, but is also variable between individuals of the same species; and it changes enormously as a tree matures. The small photographs on the right-hand page of each spread generally show the bark of a mature tree, with the caption describing changes as the tree matures.

The main photo captions describe the tree's crown shape – the crown being the top part of a tree, carrying the foliage. Crowns, like bark, vary considerably.

Shoots and buds The color and texture of shoots can be very useful for identification: see, for example, Norway maple (pages 228-229) and red maple (pages 236-237). Shoot color when described refers to the mature shoot from late summer.

The arrangement of the buds and leaves also provides useful clues. Three quarters of all broadleaved trees have them alternate along the shoot; on the rest they are in opposite pairs, apart from a few where they are in threes. Buds tend to be concentrated at the tips of shoots and the number of protective bud scales can also be a useful feature.

Beech: alternate on the shoot.

Leaves provide the easiest features. Leaf

Mountain ash and Rowan: pinnate leaves.

shape varies widely, with **pinnate** and **bi-pinnate** or twice-pinnate leaves at one extreme and simple **untoothed** leaves at the other. (Pinnate means divided into leaflets.) Some trees change leaf shape as the tree matures – see holly (pages 214-215) and California live oak and canyon live oak (pages 144-145).

At first glance, a pinnate leaf can look like a shoot with many leaves. However, there are always buds in the angle or **axil** formed between a true leaf and a shoot, but see bald-cypress (pages 40-41) and dawn-redwood (pages 38-39) which in addition have deciduous shoots without buds.

Gingko flowers.

The shape of simple leaves can vary from narrow and straight (**linear**), as in many conifers and some willows, to broader egg-shaped leaves, to leaves with marked toothing or **lobing**. The main teeth and lobes are often the ends of the lateral veins on the leaf, and leaves which have no teeth are often not as

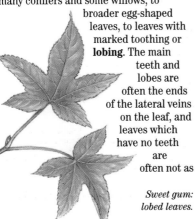

Sweet gum: lobed leaves.

heavily veined.

The term egg-shaped appears frequently in this guide to describe not just the leaves, but also some fruits. Gulliver (in Swift's *Gulliver's Travels*) may have had trouble working out which end of an egg is the bottom, but in botany the question is decided: normal egg-shaped is **ovate**, and defined as being broadest below the middle (i.e. broad end attached); while leaves which are egg-shaped but broadest above the middle are **obovate** (i.e. narrow end attached). Check with the artwork to see whether the 'egg-shape' is ovate or obovate.

Ovate.

Obovate.

The **leaf stalk** or petiole can also provide valuable characteristics, such as most cherries (pages 170-177) and London plane (pages 222-223).

Leaf stalk or petiole.

Flowers These can be very obvious when doing their stuff, which is to attract attention. However, in many trees they are rather transient, or only produced on older trees or at the tops of tall trees.

Fruits These also provide very useful characteristics. The fruit is present from the fertilization of the flower until it matures and is shed. The descriptions given provide details of the fruit, including how it changes as it ripens.

American hornbeam.

A Key to Conifers

European black pine.

Pages 14-15
Ginkgo family
Leaves broadest at the rounded tip and with many parallel veins.

Pages 16-17
Monkey puzzle family
Leaves broad at the base with a sharp point. Cones have a single seed fused to the supporting scale.

Monkey puzzle.

Conifer means 'bearing cones' – and cone refers both to the overall shape of the tree, and its fruit. But although most conifers have obvious cones and cone-shaped crowns, many do not. From a scientific viewpoint, what really defines conifers is the seeds or ovules: they are naked – in other words, not enclosed within a protective structure. This can be seen very easily with a hand-lens or magnifying glass in the female flowers of the cypresses. At the flowering stage, the small dot-like ovules are exposed between the small scales. After pollination, the scales expand and hide them. Other conifers make a better job of hiding them, even at the flowering stage, but they are always exposed to the air. This is a clear contrast with the broadleaved trees and palms, whose ovules are fully enclosed within the plant's tissues.

The conifers are an old and very diverse group, especially when ginkgo is treated as an honorary member: it actually belongs, botanically, between the ferns and the conifers.

The majority of conifers are evergreen, but tamarack (pages 46-47), dawn-redwood (pages 38-39), bald-cypress (pages 40-41) and ginkgo (pages 14-15) are deciduous. Generally, they have single trunks and light branching, forming wood which is soft and strong. This makes them desirable for timber.

Juniper.

Pages 18-33
Cypress family
Leaves generally scale like, but some juniper species (pages 32-33) have straight and narrow (linear) leaves in whorls.

The family divides into three groups on cone characteristics:

Cones with shield-like (peltate) scales, i.e. scales which have a central stalk— *Cupressus* (pages 18-23) and *Chamacyparis* (pages 24-27).

Shield-like scales.

Cones with few scales hinged at the base— *Calocedrus* (pages 28-29),
Hinged at base. *Thuja* (pages 30-31).

Cone a fleshy berry, not woody— *Juniperus* (pages 32-33).

Eastern red-cedar.

Coast redwood.

Pages 34-43
Redwood family
Leaves in flat sprays.

Pages 44-45
Yew family
Leaves in flat sprays and fruit single, with a juicy red base (aril).
  (The yew family is placed here on visual foliage character. Botanically, it belongs between ginkgo and monkey puzzle.)

Yew.

Pages 46-97
Pine family
A large and important group, in which there are two seeds to each cone scale. It consists of:

Larches (pages 46-47) and cedars (pages 48-51) whose leaves are on short spur shoots. Cones of larch are persistent, whereas in cedars the mature cone disintegrates to release the seeds and bracts.

Cedar of Lebanon.

Spruces (pages 52-59), Douglas-fir (pages 60-61), silver firs (pages 62-67) and hemlock (pages 68-69), whose foliage is in sprays with single needle leaves. Cones of silver firs break apart to scatter the seeds.
  Spruces, Douglas-fir and hemlock have cones which are woody and persistent.

Douglas-fir.

Pines (pages 70-97), have leaves in bundles of two to five.

Scots pine.

Yew.

13

Ginkgo or maidenhair tree

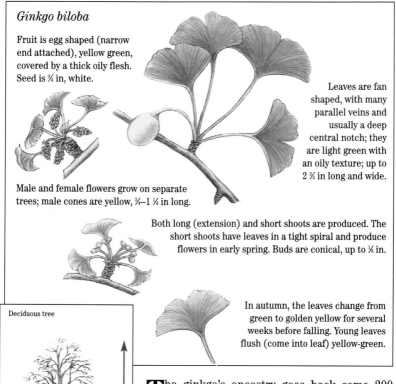

Ginkgo biloba

Fruit is egg shaped (narrow end attached), yellow green, covered by a thick oily flesh. Seed is ¾ in, white.

Leaves are fan shaped, with many parallel veins and usually a deep central notch; they are light green with an oily texture; up to 2 ¾ in long and wide.

Male and female flowers grow on separate trees; male cones are yellow, ¾–1 ¼ in long.

Both long (extension) and short shoots are produced. The short shoots have leaves in a tight spiral and produce flowers in early spring. Buds are conical, up to ⅛ in.

Deciduous tree

50–82 ft

In autumn, the leaves change from green to golden yellow for several weeks before falling. Young leaves flush (come into leaf) yellow-green.

The ginkgo's ancestry goes back some 200 million years, to before the age of dinosaurs. Fossils with similar leaves are found throughout the world. It is now only native to a remote region of eastern China and probably would have become extinct there were it not for the edible nuts. It was taken to Japan and from there to North America in the early part of the 18th century.

It is widely planted in streets or in parks and gardens for the brilliant golden yellow autumn foliage. Ginkgo is tolerant of urban conditions and long lived, with the original tree at London's Kew Gardens (planted in 1762) still thriving; but much older trees are known in the Far East. Generally, only male trees are planted, as the oily, fleshy covering to the hard seed of the female has a distinctly unpleasant odor as it decays. The alternative common name of maidenhair tree refers to the similarity of the leaves to the fronds of the maidenhair fern. Biloba refers to the two lobes of the leaves formed by the central notch, but young, vigorous trees often have more notches and thus more lobes. Botanically, ginkgo is placed between the ferns and the conifers.

With attractive foliage throughout the summer, turning bright golden yellow in the autumn, it tolerates a wide range of sites and conditions. Usually slender, with light branching when young, becoming broader in their second century.

BARK
On young trees, is gray brown with corky ridges, becoming dull gray with crossing ridges on mature trees.

Monkey puzzle

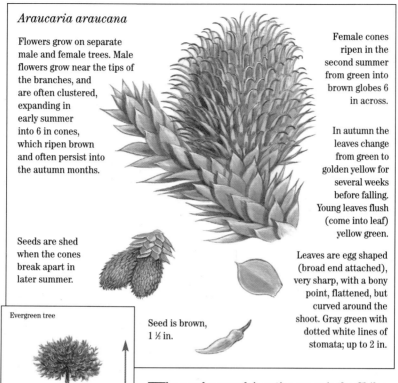

Araucaria araucana

Flowers grow on separate male and female trees. Male flowers grow near the tips of the branches, and are often clustered, expanding in early summer into 6 in cones, which ripen brown and often persist into the autumn months.

Seeds are shed when the cones break apart in later summer.

Female cones ripen in the second summer from green into brown globes 6 in across.

In autumn the leaves change from green to golden yellow for several weeks before falling. Young leaves flush (come into leaf) yellow green.

Leaves are egg shaped (broad end attached), very sharp, with a bony point, flattened, but curved around the shoot. Gray green with dotted white lines of stomata; up to 2 in.

Evergreen tree

50–100 ft

Seed is brown, 1 ½ in.

The monkey puzzle's native range is the Chilean Andes between 37 and 39 degrees south, and in adjacent parts of the Argentinean Andes. In North America it is planted as a specimen tree mainly because of its distinctive shape.

The name monkey puzzle was given at a ceremonial planting in the 1840s, and alludes to the sharp foliage, which would puzzle a climbing monkey. Araucarias were around long before monkeys, however, and date from the Jurassic period otherwise dominated by the dinosaurs. An alternative name for the species is Chile pine.

The seeds (only carried on female trees, where there is a male within pollinating distance) are very tasty, especially if roasted. The Latin name refers to the Araucano Indians, for whom the seeds were an important food source. The timber is of a high quality.

This tree is most unusual amongst conifers in being able to make suckers from the roots: old specimens are sometimes seen with a grove of suckers around them or on one side.

16

On young trees, the branching is in whorls, giving an open conical appearance, but as the trees age they become rounded at the top and denser. When growing on dry sites and where the foliage is shaded, the lower branches are lost. The bold, whorled foliage makes these unlike any other trees. They do not associate well with other species, and do best either as isolated specimens, or in groves.

BARK
Gray or dark gray, with horizontal wrinkles, which have been compared to an elephant's hide. But it may be fissured.

Italian cypress

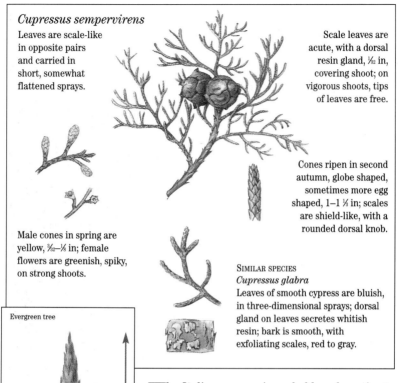

Cupressus sempervirens

Leaves are scale-like in opposite pairs and carried in short, somewhat flattened sprays.

Scale leaves are acute, with a dorsal resin gland, ⅟₃₂ in, covering shoot; on vigorous shoots, tips of leaves are free.

Cones ripen in second autumn, globe shaped, sometimes more egg shaped, 1–1 ⅛ in; scales are shield-like, with a rounded dorsal knob.

Male cones in spring are yellow, ³⁄₃₂–⅛ in; female flowers are greenish, spiky, on strong shoots.

SIMILAR SPECIES
Cupressus glabra
Leaves of smooth cypress are bluish, in three-dimensional sprays; dorsal gland on leaves secretes whitish resin; bark is smooth, with exfoliating scales, red to gray.

Evergreen tree

up to 82 ft

The Italian cypress is probably only native to the eastern Mediterranean region through to Iran. The wild form has horizontal short spreading branches. The most commonly planted form is var. *stricta*, which has erect branches making a very narrow-crowned tree, typical of regions such as Tuscany. In the wild, the tree is characteristic of limestone areas, and tolerant of long, hot dry summers. It is susceptible to a fungal disease (*Corynium* canker). This enters the scale leaves and kills the fine shoots and often larger branches. In severe cases, the tree is killed, but more often only large parts of the crown, rendering the tree unattractive, but alive. Cypresses have hard, fine wood, but it is usually not available in sufficient lengths or quantities to be commercially useful.

Smooth cypress is a tree from central Arizona. It is planted as an amenity tree for its blue-gray foliage and attractive bark. The dorsal resin glands rupture and secrete resin, which dries to a gray-white color. The cones are ½–1 in in length and the scales have forward-pointing prickles.

The 'wild' form has short spreading branches and makes a column shape when mature, but the variety *stricta*, shown here, with its very narrow tight crown of erect branches, is more commonly planted.

BARK
Gray-brown developing scaly ridges which are usually set at an angle and spiral up the trunk.

Monterey cypress

Cupressus macrocarpa

Cones, ¾–1 ½ in, ripen in the tree's second autumn but persist on tree; scales are shield-like, lumpy with a small transverse ridge.

Foliage is in dense three-dimensional sprays, which are carried erect or spreading; leaves are scale-like, ⅛₂ in, in opposite pairs which cover the shoot. They are green and acute at the tip, which is pressed down on the shoot. Dorsal resin gland is very faint and does not secrete resin.

RELATED SPECIES

Cupressus nootkatensis

Nootka cypress has foliage in flattened, drooping, possibly pendulous sprays, maybe 20 in in length. Scale leaves come in slightly unequal pairs, with the facing pair slightly shorter than the lateral pair. They are dark green, with a free bony point; dorsal resin gland is faint or absent.

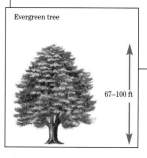

Evergreen tree

67–100 ft

Nootka cypress cones ripen in spring to summer of second year, globular, up to ½ in, with four to six pairs of scales with strong, recurved spines.

The Monterey cypress is restricted in the wild to two small coastal areas on the Monterey Peninsula of California, where the trees are small and stunted by the wind. Old trees develop very wide spreading crowns on level, tiered branches, and from a distance look similar to mature cedars of Lebanon. The combination of bright green foliage and the relatively large cones distinguish it from similar species. It is susceptible to *Corynium* canker and is usually disfigured by dead areas in the crown. The wood is resistant to decay, but not particularly strong and not usually available in marketable quantities.

Nootka cypress has a wide distribution from Northern California to southern Alaska, occurring as a mountain species. It makes a much larger tree in the wild, up to 134 ft, with bole diameters to nearly 10 ft, and produces a quality timber. Some authorities place it in the genus *Chamaecyparis*, but others think it fits better in *Cupressus*, as in this genus the cones ripen in the second year (as opposed to the first year in *Chamaecyparis*). In cultivation, Nootka cypress is mainly found as very neat conical to broad conical trees.

Young trees are conical and rather spiky, but mature trees often become very flat topped and wide spreading.

BARK
Pale brown and finely ridged on young trees, maturing pink-brown to gray and developing shallow cross-ridging on old trees.

Leyland cypress

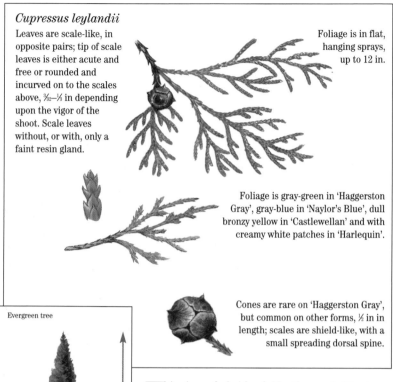

Cupressus leylandii

Leaves are scale-like, in opposite pairs; tip of scale leaves is either acute and free or rounded and incurved on to the scales above, ³⁄₃₂–⅛ in depending upon the vigor of the shoot. Scale leaves without, or with, only a faint resin gland.

Foliage is in flat, hanging sprays, up to 12 in.

Foliage is gray-green in 'Haggerston Gray', gray-blue in 'Naylor's Blue', dull bronzy yellow in 'Castlewellan' and with creamy white patches in 'Harlequin'.

Cones are rare on 'Haggerston Gray', but common on other forms, ½ in in length; scales are shield-like, with a small spreading dorsal spine.

Evergreen tree

82–131 ft

This is a hybrid of Nootka and Monterey cypresses. Although the two trees are both from western North America, they do not meet in the wild, and the hybrid has only occurred in the British Isles. It is closest to Nootka cypress. Its hybrid vigor or 'heterosis' is well known among gardeners and it grows much faster than either parent. As a result, it has replaced Monterey cypress as a hedging plant, to the fury of many a neighbor. It withstands trimming, and will grow 2 ½–3 ft a year; trimmed a couple of times a year, it creates a useful hedge or screen. However, there are better trees from which to form hedges, more forgiving if not trimmed regularly: these include yew, which is not much slower to make a neat hedge. *Cupressus leylandii* does not set seed and is propagated from cuttings. The most attractive form is 'Naylor Blue', whose gray-blue foliage is especially pretty when the sun comes out after a shower.

'Castlewellan' is a seedling of the golden or 'Lutea' form of Monterey cypress but has rather dull bronze-colored foliage. 'Harlequin' and 'Silver Dust' are two variegated forms of 'Haggerston Gray' fit for firewood.

Usually seen as a line or overgrown hedge, but can be attractive as a specimen free-standing tree. Shown here is the commonest form of *Cupressus leylandii*, the clone 'Haggerston Gray', which is the easiest to root from the cuttings.

BARK
Smooth and green-brown on young trees, on older trees becoming dark brown and developing shallow, stringy ridges.

Port Orford cedar

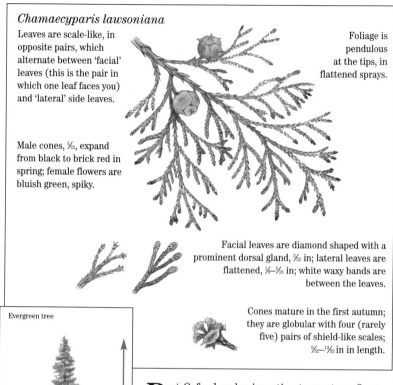

Chamaecyparis lawsoniana

Leaves are scale-like, in opposite pairs, which alternate between 'facial' leaves (this is the pair in which one leaf faces you) and 'lateral' side leaves.

Foliage is pendulous at the tips, in flattened sprays.

Male cones, ⁵⁄₆₂, expand from black to brick red in spring; female flowers are bluish green, spiky.

Facial leaves are diamond shaped with a prominent dorsal gland, ³⁄₆₂ in; lateral leaves are flattened, ⅛–⁵⁄₁₆ in; white waxy bands are between the leaves.

Cones mature in the first autumn; they are globular with four (rarely five) pairs of shield-like scales; ⁹⁄₃₂–¹³⁄₃₂ in in length.

Evergreen tree

50–67 ft

Port Orford cedar is native to western Oregon and Northern California, where it forms large trees growing up to 167–200 ft by 7 ft, usually associated with species such as Douglas fir. The timber is light, soft and commercially useful. The tree is susceptible to root death caused by *Phytophthora*, single-celled yeast-like fungi which utilize the free sugars in the roots, thereby killing the tree. It is a waterborne disease and easily spread by wet soil on car tires. The disease is decimating the wild population and will kill trees in gardens, which are then available to be colonized by honey fungus. The fungus, with its large fruit bodies and ability to digest wood, is then blamed for killing the tree.

The species was named after William Lawson, an Edinburgh nurseryman who first grew it from seeds collected in Oregon in 1854. Soon after it was introduced it gave rise to cultivars and now there are several hundred forms. Some are dwarf forms or have colored foliage, others remain as neat cones or columns, but I particularly like those which develop a crown with erratically spreading branches as they mature.

Chamaecyparis lawsoniana is used as a specimen tree, as a screen or hedging. There are a large number of garden selections, including tree forms; golden forms (such as *'Stewartii'*); blue forms (such as 'Pembury Blue'); and forms in which the juvenile pointed foliage persists (*'Ellwoodii'* and *'Fletcheri'*). There are also innumerable dwarf to slow-growing selections.

BARK
Shiny, smooth gray-green on young trees, becoming purple brown or red brown with fissures and fibrous ridges on old trees.

Sawara falsecypress

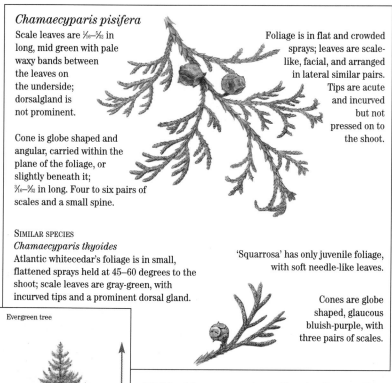

Chamaecyparis pisifera

Scale leaves are ⅟₁₆–⁵⁄₃₂ in long, mid green with pale waxy bands between the leaves on the underside; dorsalgland is not prominent.

Foliage is in flat and crowded sprays; leaves are scale-like, facial, and arranged in lateral similar pairs. Tips are acute and incurved but not pressed on to the shoot.

Cone is globe shaped and angular, carried within the plane of the foliage, or slightly beneath it; ³⁄₁₆–⁵⁄₃₂ in long. Four to six pairs of scales and a small spine.

SIMILAR SPECIES
Chamaecyparis thyoides
Atlantic whitecedar's foliage is in small, flattened sprays held at 45–60 degrees to the shoot; scale leaves are gray-green, with incurved tips and a prominent dorsal gland.

'Squarrosa' has only juvenile foliage, with soft needle-like leaves.

Cones are globe shaped, glaucous bluish-purple, with three pairs of scales.

Evergreen tree

50 ft

This falsecypress is native to the southern Japanese islands of Honshu and Kyushu, where it is one of the important timber trees because of its light, soft wood. In Europe, it is cultivated as an ornamental. The cultivar 'Aurea' is closest to the wild type, differing in the bright gold new foliage, which persists as yellow-green. 'Plumosa' has partly juvenile foliage: the leaves are needle-like, but the free tips are only ³⁄₃₂–⁵⁄₃₂ in, and yellowish gray-green. 'Squarrosa' has fully juvenile bluish foliage, with the free tips to the leaves ³⁄₁₆–⁹⁄₃₂ in long. 'Boulevard' is a form of 'Squarrosa' with much brighter foliage when growing well. Unfortunately, except on the very best moist sites, 'Boulevard' rarely grows well except in the nurseries, and in most gardens it gets moth-eaten.

Atlantic whitecedar comes from eastern U.S.A. from Maine to Georgia (but a related species occurs from Florida to Mississippi), where it grows on wetland sites. It makes a small tree, rarely more than 33 ft high. In cultivation, it is mainly represented by three cultivars, 'Andelyensis', 'Glauca' and 'Variegata', whose foliage has large splashes of yellow.

Chamaecyparis pisifera has given rise to a number of cultivars which are used as garden ornamentals, such as this fine example of the golden form, *Filifera aurea*.

BARK
Reddish-brown or gray, initially smooth, but becoming deeply fissured with broad, slightly peeling ridges.

Incense-cedar

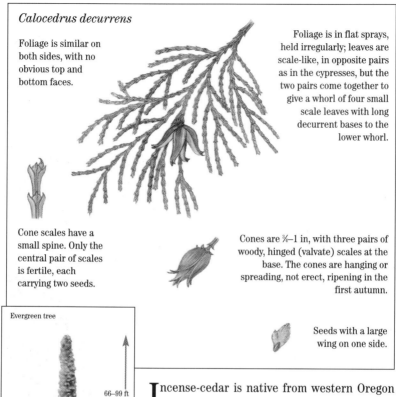

Calocedrus decurrens

Foliage is similar on both sides, with no obvious top and bottom faces.

Foliage is in flat sprays, held irregularly; leaves are scale-like, in opposite pairs as in the cypresses, but the two pairs come together to give a whorl of four small scale leaves with long decurrent bases to the lower whorl.

Cone scales have a small spine. Only the central pair of scales is fertile, each carrying two seeds.

Cones are ¾–1 in, with three pairs of woody, hinged (valvate) scales at the base. The cones are hanging or spreading, not erect, ripening in the first autumn.

Evergreen tree

66–99 ft

Seeds with a large wing on one side.

Incense-cedar is native from western Oregon south to Baja California in northern Mexico and inland to western Nevada. Over this range, it has a broadly conical crown, with strong level branching, quite different from the usual narrow crowned form cultivated in Europe. Recently a remote population in northern Oregon to the east of Mount Hood has been found. It has much shorter branches and the crown is column shaped.

The common name derives from the fragrant and durable timber. It is soft, and can be worked with and across the grain, which makes it particularly useful for pencils. Incense-cedar is tolerant of a range of sites and conditions, and of honey fungus and *Phytophthora*, making it suitable for situations where these present a problem. The bark is usually thick and ridged, but some trees in the wild have attractive, flaky, scaly bark. The cones show a relationship with *Thuja*, but the important differences between the two genera are that on *Thuja* the cone has two to three pairs of fertile scales, the seeds have two equal wings, and the cones are carried more or less erect on the foliage sprays.

The tree illustrated is growing in a remote population to the east of Mount Hood (see opposite). This population has much shorter branching and makes a much narrower tree than found in the populations to the south and west. It is growing in a forest of *Pinus ponderosa* (see page 88), which is typical of *Calocedrus decurrens* forming part of a mixed conifer forest.

BARK
Smooth gray and purple when young. Older trees become red brown and furrowed or scaly, with flaking scales.

Western red-cedar

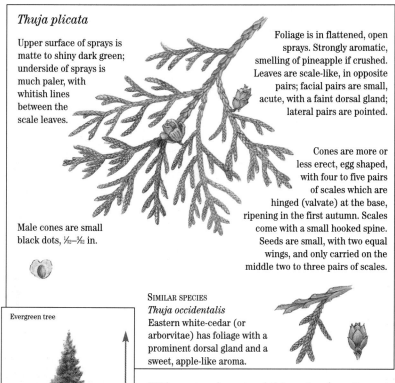

Thuja plicata

Upper surface of sprays is matte to shiny dark green; underside of sprays is much paler, with whitish lines between the scale leaves.

Foliage is in flattened, open sprays. Strongly aromatic, smelling of pineapple if crushed. Leaves are scale-like, in opposite pairs; facial pairs are small, acute, with a faint dorsal gland; lateral pairs are pointed.

Cones are more or less erect, egg shaped, with four to five pairs of scales which are hinged (valvate) at the base, ripening in the first autumn. Scales come with a small hooked spine. Seeds are small, with two equal wings, and only carried on the middle two to three pairs of scales.

Male cones are small black dots, ⅟₃₂–³⁄₃₂ in.

SIMILAR SPECIES
Thuja occidentalis
Eastern white-cedar (or arborvitae) has foliage with a prominent dorsal gland and a sweet, apple-like aroma.

Evergreen tree

84–167 ft

The natural range of this cedar (an alternate name is giant arborvitae) is the Pacific coast of North America from southern Alaska to Northern California, also inland on the east side of the Rocky Mountains from interior British Columbia to northern Idaho. The wood is soft, easily worked, naturally durable, and familiar as the red-brown timber used for structures such as sheds or conservatories; also for roofing shingles and the cladding of modern bungalows. The Native Americans used it for canoes and totem poles. The common name derives from the red hue of the wood. In cultivation, the tree is used as an ornamental, and in forestry. It is a fast-growing tree and tolerates a wide range of sites, from dry sands, chalk and limestone to wet places.

Eastern white-cedar is a much smaller and slower-growing tree from eastern North America. The name 'arborvitae', or 'tree of life', is derived from the high vitamin C content of the foliage which was used by early explorers to prevent or cure scurvy. The cone is egg shaped, yellow-green to brown, and the scales are smooth, without a dorsal prickle.

Thuja plicata makes a tall tree with a trunk which is heavily buttressed and swollen at the base. The short spreading branches will be retained to ground level in open sites, but in dense woodland will be lost.

BARK
Red-brown and fissured, with narrow strips which often lift off; base of trunk is often fluted and expanded.

Eastern red-cedar

Juniperus virginiana

Foliage is in two different types. Adult foliage is decussate (that is, opposite pairs, with the alternate pairs at right angles to the ones above and below), colored gray-green or dark gray with small, egg shaped leaves less than $\frac{1}{10}$ in. It is tightly pressed to the stem. Juvenile leaves are needle-like, in pairs, up to $\frac{1}{2}$ in long, gray-green on the convex outer face, waxy bluish-white (glaucous) on the convex inner face. Often, though, some juvenile leaves are seen at the base and tip of a shoot with adult leaves.

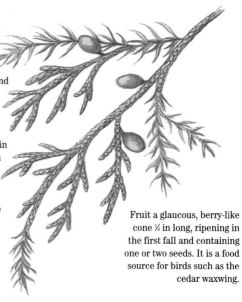

Fruit a glaucous, berry-like cone $\frac{1}{4}$ in long, ripening in the first fall and containing one or two seeds. It is a food source for birds such as the cedar waxwing.

Evergreen tree

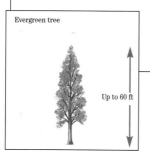

Up to 60 ft

Eastern red-cedar is found in the East from Maine across to southern Ontario and North Dakota, and from there south to central Texas and just into northern Florida. It does not occur on the coastal plain in the Southeast, where there is a smaller related juniper, *Juniperus silicola*. It grows on a wide range of soils and sites, from dry upland limestone areas to floodplains and swamps. Such places are likely to be low in nitrogen, thereby allowing it to compete against faster-growing hardwoods such as oaks and hickories.

Eastern red-cedar is neither a cedar (which is the genus *Cedrus*, although the common name is frequently used for any conifer with a durable and fragrant wood), nor is it related to the western red-cedar, which is *Thuja plicata*. The wood is easily worked and is durable, bright red and thus also called 'red juniper'. It has appeared in cabinets, but its special use is for pencils—the British name for it being pencil cedar. The wood yields cedar oil, used in perfumes and medicine.

Juniperus virginiana usually makes a dense and rather narrow column shaped crown, less often becoming broader.

BARK
Gray-brown or red-brown, with fibrous spiral ridges which tend to strip away slightly.

33

Giant sequoia

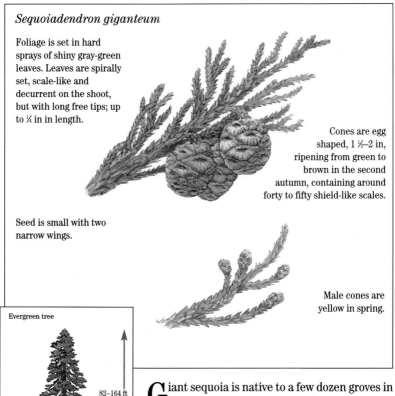

Sequoiadendron giganteum

Foliage is set in hard sprays of shiny gray-green leaves. Leaves are spirally set, scale-like and decurrent on the shoot, but with long free tips; up to ¼ in in length.

Cones are egg shaped, 1 ½–2 in, ripening from green to brown in the second autumn, containing around forty to fifty shield-like scales.

Seed is small with two narrow wings.

Male cones are yellow in spring.

Evergreen tree

82–164 ft

Giant sequoia is native to a few dozen groves in the Sierra Nevada mountains of eastern California. The largest of all the trees has been named 'General Sherman': it has a bole diameter of 33 ft, is 284 ft in height and has been estimated to weigh 6,000 tons. Yet, like all of its kind, it grew from a seed weighing about ¹⁄₂₀₀ of an ounce. The bark may be 12 in or more thick in old trees. It is soft and fibrous, but noticeably harder than the bark of *Sequoia*. Fibrous and easily excavated, it provides winter niches for small birds. The timber is brittle and of low quality, and so is not harvested.

The species first came to notice in 1854, after the death of the Duke of Wellington: a British botanist named it *Wellingtonia gigantea* in his honor. However, in a touch which would have pleased Napoleon, a Frenchman had earlier named an African genus after the Duke, so *Wellingtonia gigantea* could not stand as the botanical name. So it was placed in the genus *Sequoia*. There it stayed, long enough for the U.S. Congress to create the Sequoia National Park in order to preserve it. Later it was placed in a genus of its own.

In the wild, *Sequoiadendron giganteum* forms impressive groves of enormous trees, which defy 'whole tree' photography and are often without live branches for the first 50 or 100 ft. When grown as a specimen tree, the branches are retained to ground level.

BARK
Red-brown and very thick, quickly developing deep ridges, often with small cup shaped hollows caused by sheltering birds.

Coast redwood

Sequoia sempervirens

Leaves are linear, acute at the tip and tapering to the base, which is decurrent on the shoot, matte green above, silvery gray in two bands beneath.

Foliage is in flat sprays, with leaves set on both sides of the shoot, like the teeth of a comb; the longest leaves, up to ¾ in long, are in the center of the shoot.

Cones ripen in early autumn, are rounded oblong, with about twenty shield-like scales, ½–1 ¼ in long.

Evergreen tree

66–164 ft or more

The coast redwood or sequoia is restricted in the wild to coastal California from just north of San Francisco into the southwestern tip of Oregon: in other words, to the fog belt of the California coast. Indeed, the tree is believed to receive a significant proportion of its water needs from intercepting fog. Quite how it manages to transport water and nutrients from the roots to the top of the tree is not known. The tallest tree is 374 ft; a column of water this high would weigh more than eleven times atmospheric pressure. The very tallest trees are in valley bottoms, where periodic flooding kills competing trees. The very thick bark is also a protection against forest fires. Coast redwood's alternative names, *sequoia* or redwood, differentiate it from *Sequoiadendron* (page 34). The generic name is after Sequoiah, son of a British trader and a Cherokee woman, credited with inventing an alphabet for the Cherokee language. As both *Sequoiadendron* (page 34) and *Metasequoia* (page 38) are named for their affinity to *Sequoia*, Sequoiah has three tree genera named after him. Yet there is no evidence that he saw any of them.

Sequoia sempervirens is one of the few conifers which produce sprout shoots at the base. The wood is excellent, used for sawn timber in house-building.

BARK
Red-brown, extremely thick with deep ridges, fibrous and very soft.

Dawn-redwood

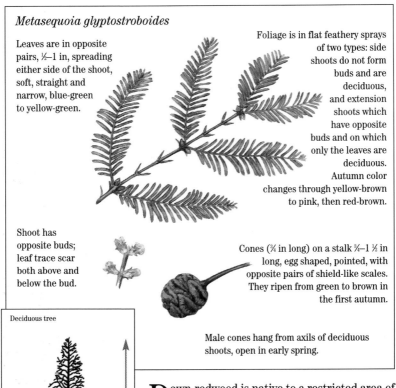

Metasequoia glyptostroboides

Leaves are in opposite pairs, ½–1 in, spreading either side of the shoot, soft, straight and narrow, blue-green to yellow-green.

Foliage is in flat feathery sprays of two types: side shoots do not form buds and are deciduous, and extension shoots which have opposite buds and on which only the leaves are deciduous. Autumn color changes through yellow-brown to pink, then red-brown.

Shoot has opposite buds; leaf trace scar both above and below the bud.

Cones (¾ in long) on a stalk ¾–1 ½ in long, egg shaped, pointed, with opposite pairs of shield-like scales. They ripen from green to brown in the first autumn.

Male cones hang from axils of deciduous shoots, open in early spring.

Deciduous tree

66–100 ft

Dawn-redwood is native to a restricted area of Hubei and Sichuan Provinces in central China. However, there are well-preserved specimens in the Canadian Arctic dated as 50 million years old, and fossils in coal from many places in the Northern Hemisphere indicate that it was widespread. The surviving trees in China were only found in the 1940s and introduced to the U.S.A. in 1948. The local Chinese name is water fir, which conjures up the boggy sites to which the tree has been restricted in the wild. However, while dawn-redwood is happy to grow with its feet (and ankles) in water, it is happiest in a moist, deep soil and tolerates some dryish sites. Best growth has occurred on Long Island, New York, and in Delaware and Pennsylvania. This versatility has turned it into a popular amenity tree, greatly helped by the luxuriant foliage and attractive autumn color. The shoots in winter are unique for the double scars around the buds. The buds are carried in a leaf axil and the scar beneath the bud is made when the leaf falls. The deciduous shoots are formed just above the buds and the upper scar is caused when they fall.

The feathery foliage on *Metasequoia glyptostroboides's* pleasing cone shaped crown makes an attractive tree all year.

BARK
Orange-brown to red-brown, on young trees smooth, but soon developing papery scales, then fibrous with stringy ridges. Trunk is often fluted at the base.

Bald-cypress

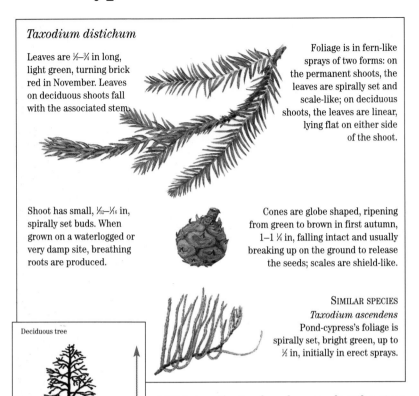

Taxodium distichum

Leaves are ½–¾ in long, light green, turning brick red in November. Leaves on deciduous shoots fall with the associated stem.

Foliage is in fern-like sprays of two forms: on the permanent shoots, the leaves are spirally set and scale-like; on deciduous shoots, the leaves are linear, lying flat on either side of the shoot.

Shoot has small, ½₂–⅟₁₆ in, spirally set buds. When grown on a waterlogged or very damp site, breathing roots are produced.

Cones are globe shaped, ripening from green to brown in first autumn, 1–1¼ in, falling intact and usually breaking up on the ground to release the seeds; scales are shield-like.

SIMILAR SPECIES
Taxodium ascendens
Pond-cypress's foliage is spirally set, bright green, up to ½ in, initially in erect sprays.

Deciduous tree

49–82 ft

This is native to a broad sweep of southeastern U.S.A. from New Jersey to Texas and up the Mississippi Valley. It is characteristic of wet bottomland sites and thrives on periodic flooding. Although it can grow in permanent swamps, it is best suited to moist, well-drained sites. However, it cannot compete in such places with faster-growing broadleaved trees; whereas on flooded sites, its pneumatophores or 'knees' solve the problem of getting oxygen to the roots to allow them to respire, sometimes 60 ft from the parent tree. (Pneumatophores, illustrated in bark photo, are stubby structures which rise above soil level.) Bald-cypress is also called swamp-cypress.

Pond-cypress is found in the wild from Virginia to Louisiana, but generally at low levels and around ponds rather than rivers. The leaves are scale-like on the deciduous shoots, and the tree very rarely produces knees. The botanical name refers to the ascending new foliage, but it droops by autumn. Pond-cypress is sometimes treated as a variety of bald-cypress, as *T. distichum* var. *imbricarium*.

Taxodium distichum is well adapted to wet places, but is also perfectly happy on dry sites. Young trees are conical. Shown here is an old tree with a spreading crown.

BARK
Dull brown to reddish-brown, later fissured and, on older trees, peeling in narrow strips.

Japanese cedar

Cryptomeria japonica

Leaves are needle-like, soft and incurved, mid to dark green, with two whitish bands, up to ¾ in long, with the longest leaves in the middle part of the shoot.

Foliage is in three-dimensional sprays, set radially around the shoot in five rows.

Cones are globe shaped, ripening from green to brown in first autumn, with twenty to thirty scales. Scales are shield-like, with a dorsal recurved spine and three to five erect, triangular teeth.

Male cones develop in spring in the axils of leaves near the tips of last year's shoots. They are ⁵⁄₃₂–⁵⁄₁₆ in long, egg shaped to oblong, and yellow-green.

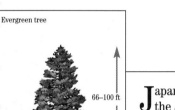

Evergreen tree

66–100 ft

Japanese cedar is native to the southern part of the Japanese archipelago, but because it has been used in forestry throughout Japan for many centuries, its true native area is obscured by planting. Very stout old trees remain on the small southern Islet of Yakushima. It is one of the few conifers which will coppice, meaning regrow from the stump if cut down. It has a light, soft timber similar to that of the redwoods.

At least as common in cultivation is *elegans*. This is a fixed juvenile form in which the leaves are longer, more widely spaced and softer. It can make a tree up to 100 ft high, but usually grows at an angle to the vertical. Cones are produced, but it is one of the easiest trees to root from cuttings. *Cryptomeria* also occurs in China south of the Yangtze River, where it is grown for its timber. Some treat this tree as a separate species, variety or form of Japanese cedar. It is marked out by its attractive, fresh, green, soft foliage, which tends to hang down more than the Japanese forms. However, it is not impossible that it was an early introduction from Japan.

Young *Cryptomeria japonicas* are cone shaped, but older ones have a rounded crown with spaced branches.

BARK
Red-brown or orange-brown. Young trees exfoliate in small flakes; older trees have a thick, fibrous bark, which peels in long strips.

Pacific yew

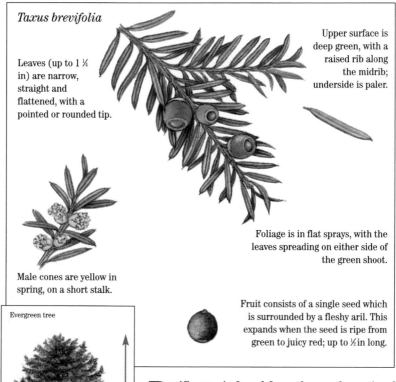

Taxus brevifolia

Leaves (up to 1 ¼ in) are narrow, straight and flattened, with a pointed or rounded tip.

Upper surface is deep green, with a raised rib along the midrib; underside is paler.

Foliage is in flat sprays, with the leaves spreading on either side of the green shoot.

Male cones are yellow in spring, on a short stalk.

Fruit consists of a single seed which is surrounded by a fleshy aril. This expands when the seed is ripe from green to juicy red; up to ½ in long.

Evergreen tree

50–65 ft

Pacific yew is found from the southern tip of Alaska along the coast to central California, where it also occurs in the northern Sierra Nevada. It is also in the Rocky Mountains of southeastern British Columbia, eastern Washington to northeastern Oregon and northwest Montana and central Idaho. It prefers moist sites, such as stream sides and in canyon bottoms.

English yew (*Taxus baccata*), its close relative, is cultivated in North America especially in parks and gardens. It is not fully hardy in the Midwest or in northern New England. In these areas it is replaced as a landscape tree or shrub either by Japanese yew (*Taxus cuspidata*) or their hybrid *T. media*, also called Anglojap yew. Japanese yew has more irregularly arranged foliage which is usually dark lustrous green above with yellow-green bands on the underside. The new growth is a soft yellow-green. All yews contain alkaloids in their leaves, shoots, bark, wood and seeds. This does not stop deer or moose burrowing in them, but cattle and people can be killed by eating small quantities. The wood is very hard and durable, with beautiful veining, and is used for bows and paddles.

Taxus brevifolia is usually seen as scattered trees, whether in the open or as understory trees in conifer forest. As a landscape tree it is valued for the habit as well as for the dense evergreen foliage.

BARK
Smooth purplish-brown on young trees; on older ones, the bark develops scales which flake off to show red-brown, purple or yellow patches.

Tamarack

Larix laricina

Leaves ¾–1 ¼ in long, in clusters of fifteen–thirty. They are straight and narrow, with a diamond cross-section. Bluish-green or dark green above, with two pale bands beneath.

Shoot is orange-brown, with a waxy pink-gray bloom in the first winter. It is prominently ridged at the base of fallen needles. Globe shaped, resinous, red-brown buds.

Egg shaped (ovoid) to nearly round cones ripen to light brown in first autumn. They are ½–¾ in long, with up to twenty scales. Bract scales are just visible between the basal seed scales only.

SIMILAR SPECIES
Larix decidua
European larch's shoots are a shiny straw yellow, becoming yellow-brown over winter.

Green leaves in rosettes of thirty to forty on spur shoots. Up to 1 ½ in long, soft, straight and narrow. The one-year shoots give a yellow haze to the trees in winter.

Cone is erect, conical or cylindrical, 1 ½–¾ in. It has rounded, woody scales and the bract is seen between the lowest scales only.

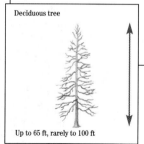

Deciduous tree

Up to 65 ft, rarely to 100 ft

Tamarack extends right across the continent, from the Atlantic coast of Labrador and Newfoundland almost to the Bering Sea in central Alaska. In the U.S.A. it is restricted to the states north of a line between Wisconsin to New Jersey, although there are a few scattered populations in northern West Virginia. It extends to the northern limit of tree growth.

The tree can grow on swampy sites, and is often restricted to these situations along the southern edge of its range. However, it thrives best on better-drained upland sites. On bogs, and at the northern limit of tree growth, it is often more of a shrub than a tree. It forms either pure forests or is associated with other conifers, especially black spruce. It requires full light.

Tamarack timber is resinous: unsuitable for pulp, but durable as lumber. The resin and its thin bark make it susceptible to forest fires. The slender roots were used by Native Americans to sew sheets of birch together when making canoes. European larch is planted for timber and has naturalized in parts of northeastern U.S.A.

Larix laricina has a
slender conical crown
with horizontal branches.

BARK
Red-brown and scaly in old
trees, but smooth and thin
in young trees.

Cedar of Lebanon

Cedrus libani

Foliage is helical on long shoots, but in rosettes of ten to twenty leaves. These are retained two to three years until thirty to sixty leaves have grown on erect, short shoots. Leaves are four-sided, ¾–1 in, gray-green with white lines on all four sides, and a bony point at the apex.

Cone is barrel shaped, 3–5 in, maturing to brown in first autumn and breaking apart over the next year to release the seeds and bract scales, leaving a spiky stalk on the shoot.

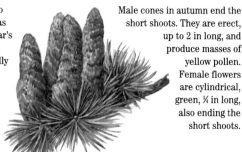

SIMILAR SPECIES
Cedrus atlantica

Atlas cedar's foliage is similar to that of cedar of Lebanon, but has more leaves (30–45) in each year's growth on the short shoots. The leaves are ½–1 in long and usually covered by wax, making the foliage blue or silvery.

Male cones in autumn end the short shoots. They are erect, up to 2 in long, and produce masses of yellow pollen. Female flowers are cylindrical, green, ¾ in long, also ending the short shoots.

Evergreen tree

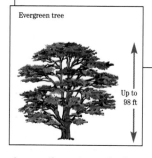

Up to 98 ft

Cedar of Lebanon, a popular ornamental tree in American parks, occurs wild in a small number of stands restricted to the western side of the Lebanon Mountains, where they receive rainfall from the Mediterranean. It also occurs in northwestern Syria and in southern Turkey, where the trees do not develop the typical broad, flat-topped crowns with foliage held horizontally. It has a fragrant and durable light timber which has been used over the millennia for building: witness the famous temple in Jerusalem which was built by King Solomon nearly three thousand years ago.

Atlas cedar is restricted to the Atlas Mountains of Morocco and Algeria, where it still forms forests. It is mainly cultivated as the blue foliage form, but, in the wild, trees with green foliage are common. Both cedars are especially tolerant of chalky soil. What they don't like is shade—they need full sunlight to look their best. Cedar of Lebanon was introduced in colonial times but Atlas cedar arrived in the 1840s. Atlas cedar is more attractive as a young tree, but perhaps without the poise of a mature cedar of Lebanon.

Cedrus libani develops horizontal flat-topped branches, as here, but young trees are spiky. The drawback to flat branches is their tendency to break under the weight of wet snow.

BARK
Dark gray or brown and smooth on young trees, becoming blackish and developing scaly ridges on old trees.

Deodar cedar

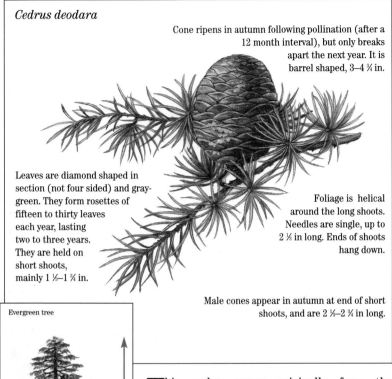

Cedrus deodara

Cone ripens in autumn following pollination (after a 12 month interval), but only breaks apart the next year. It is barrel shaped, 3–4 ¾ in.

Leaves are diamond shaped in section (not four sided) and gray-green. They form rosettes of fifteen to thirty leaves each year, lasting two to three years. They are held on short shoots, mainly 1 ⅕–1 ¾ in.

Foliage is helical around the long shoots. Needles are single, up to 2 ⅛ in long. Ends of shoots hang down.

Male cones appear in autumn at end of short shoots, and are 2 ⅛–2 ¾ in long.

Evergreen tree

Up to 131 ft

This cedar comes originally from the northwestern part of the Indian subcontinent, from western Nepal through to eastern Afghanistan. It makes an attractive amenity tree, but tends to look best as a young tree, when it grows vigorously, with a narrow crown and branch tips that hang down noticeably. Older trees only look good when they are growing on a moist site, otherwise they tend to become rather ragged, with dieback. It does not form the level, tiered branches characteristic of cedar of Lebanon. While cedar of Lebanon needs to be 50 years old to look its best, and Atlas cedar 15 to 20 years, deodars can be very attractive up to 20 years. Ideally, a replacement tree should be planted before the older tree is felled, but this is not the average gardener's idea of managing trees.

Deodar and *deodara* are derived from the Indian name for the species. Like the other cedars, it has a useful timber. In cultivation, all the true cedars (those which belong to the genus *Cedrus*) will hybridize, but deodar is the most distinctive one.

Cedrus deodara makes an attractive ornamental tree, largely because of its hanging branches.

BARK
On young trees, smooth and gray, but this fissures to give wide black to pinkish-gray furrows and short scaly ridges.

Norway spruce

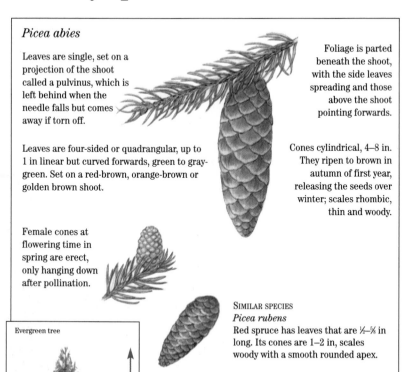

Picea abies

Leaves are single, set on a projection of the shoot called a pulvinus, which is left behind when the needle falls but comes away if torn off.

Foliage is parted beneath the shoot, with the side leaves spreading and those above the shoot pointing forwards.

Leaves are four-sided or quadrangular, up to 1 in linear but curved forwards, green to gray-green. Set on a red-brown, orange-brown or golden brown shoot.

Cones cylindrical, 4–8 in. They ripen to brown in autumn of first year, releasing the seeds over winter; scales rhombic, thin and woody.

Female cones at flowering time in spring are erect, only hanging down after pollination.

SIMILAR SPECIES
Picea rubens
Red spruce has leaves that are ½–⅝ in long. Its cones are 1–2 in, scales woody with a smooth rounded apex.

Evergreen tree

82–131 ft

Norway spruce is found throughout Europe, but only just extends into southern Norway. In North America it is used in shelterbelts, forestry plantations, as a landscape tree (especially in northeastern U.S.A.) and as a Christmas tree. It has become naturalized in places, including Minnesota, parts of the New England and in regions of Canada. It has a white timber of good quality and is used in building, for paper pulp and for the sounding boards of violins—in fact some call it violin wood. It can be attractive when well grown, but almost any other spruce would be just as good in the same conditions.

Red spruce occurs from New Brunswick and Prince Edward Island south to eastern Tennessee and western North Carolina in the Appalachians. It is restricted to mountaintop sites at the southern end of this range, but is more widely distributed in the north. In upland New England and New York it is the commonest spruce. It occurs either in pure stands or mixed with other conifers or broadleaved trees, and grows on both well drained and poorly drained swampy sites.

Picea abies makes a neat and pleasing landscape specimen because it keeps its foliage down to ground level.

BARK
Red-brown and finely flaky in young trees, becoming scaly at the base and purple or gray in old trees.

Sitka spruce

Picea sitchensis

Leaves are linear, diamond shaped in section, drawn out at the tip to a sharp bony point, ¾–1 in; upper surface is deep shiny green with no white bands or with two narrow white bands; underside has two gray-green or bluish bands.

Foliage is parted beneath the shoot, spreading at the sides and loosely pressed down along the top of the shoot.

Cones are cylindrical, ripening pale brown or whitish in first autumn, 2–4 in; scales are thin, stiff with a jaggedly toothed margin.

SIMILAR SPECIES
Picea glauca

White spruce's foliage tends to be arranged more above the shoot than below; leaves curve forwards, are diamond shaped in section, bluish green with white lines on all four sides, ⅛–¼ in.

White spruce's cones are narrow, egg shaped, tapering to both ends, 1–2 ½ in; scales are rounded, thin, woody and finely toothed.

Evergreen tree

82–197 ft

In its natural range, Sitka spruce is found from Northern California up to Alaska along the Pacific coast of North America. It is a species of the coastal temperate rain forest belt and only found within 8750 yd of the sea. One of its American names is tideland spruce; the common name refers to Sitka in southern Alaska. The species needs plenty of rainfall and in the wild is not found on sites which dry out. It tolerates wind and exposure, although on shallow soils it is likely to be uprooted by strong winds. The timber is strong and useful, both for sawlogs and for pulp, and the tree is planted for forestry.

White spruce and black spruce occur from inland Alaska across to the Atlantic seaboard of Canada, only extending into mainland US around the Great Lakes and in New England. White spruce is smaller and slower growing than Sitka spruce and like with this species, the cones fall off soon after opening to release the seeds in the fall. Black spruce has short (¼–⅝ in) ashy blue-green needles. The cones are egg shaped, up to 1 ¼ in, and persist for a year or more after opening. It occurs in bogs, or in mixed stands on better soils.

Picea sitchensis is attractive as an individual tree, as here, showing the silvery undersides. Older trees develop stout boles with buttressed roots. When grown in the open, the lower branches are kept but in woodland these are lost, leaving a long clear trunk.

BARK
Purplish-brown on young trees, becoming grayer on old trees and developing scales which flake off in concave plates, especially in the lower trunk.

Blue spruce

Picea pungens

Leaves vary from gray-green to vivid blue depending upon the quantity of wax which covers them. Older leaves lose the wax and become greener.

Foliage mainly spreads at the sides and is raised up above the shoot; leaves are curved, four sided, almost square in section, tapering to a sharp bony point; ½–1 in long.

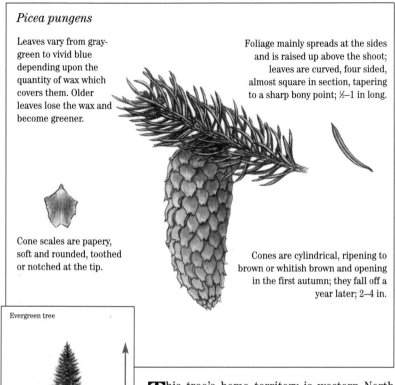

Cone scales are papery, soft and rounded, toothed or notched at the tip.

Cones are cylindrical, ripening to brown or whitish brown and opening in the first autumn; they fall off a year later; 2–4 in.

Evergreen tree

50–82 ft

This tree's home territory is western North America from Wyoming and Idaho south to New Mexico, Arizona and Colorado. This is a relatively dry part of the continent and the tree is restricted either to small stands along streams, or to north-facing slopes where evaporation is least. Both green and blue foliaged forms occur in the wild, but it is the bluest forms which have been selected by nurserymen and make the overwhelming majority of trees sold in North America. At their best, the blue forms can be quite impressive, especially as young trees, but they tend to suffer in several ways. The tree needs plenty of moisture to grow really well, but often fails to achieve this as towns are often in drier areas. The foliage loses its attractive waxy layer as it ages, and becomes green. Also, the very intensity of the most blue forms can detract from other plant combinations. Grabbing hold of the foliage can also be painful: there are sharp, bony points in the stout needles.

This spruce is the state tree of Colorado, as Colorado blue spruce, but elsewhere is usually called blue spruce (including Utah where it is also the state tree).

Picea pungens makes a broadly
conical tree, occasionally to 150 ft,
in its native stands where green
foliage trees occur with blue
specimens. In gardens, it is the
blue form which predominates,
making a smaller tree.

BARK
Red-brown or purple-gray,
developing scaly plates
which flake off.

Brewer's spruce

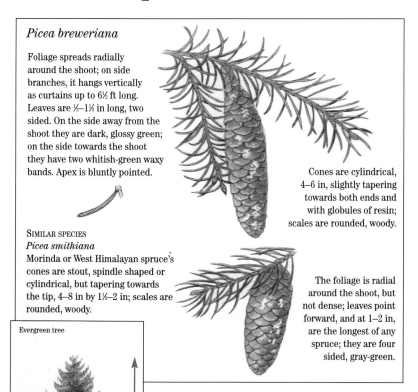

Picea breweriana

Foliage spreads radially around the shoot; on side branches, it hangs vertically as curtains up to 6½ ft long. Leaves are ½–1¼ in long, two sided. On the side away from the shoot they are dark, glossy green; on the side towards the shoot they have two whitish-green waxy bands. Apex is bluntly pointed.

SIMILAR SPECIES
Picea smithiana
Morinda or West Himalayan spruce's cones are stout, spindle shaped or cylindrical, but tapering towards the tip, 4–8 in by 1½–2 in; scales are rounded, woody.

Cones are cylindrical, 4–6 in, slightly tapering towards both ends and with globules of resin; scales are rounded, woody.

The foliage is radial around the shoot, but not dense; leaves point forward, and at 1–2 in, are the longest of any spruce; they are four sided, gray-green.

Evergreen tree

33–66 ft

Brewer's spruce is restricted in the wild to the Siskiyou Mountains of southwestern Oregon and Northern California in a region which escaped being glaciated in the most recent Ice Age. It occurs with pines, silver firs and Douglas fir. It can grow beyond 164 ft with a 3 ft bole diameter. Its curtains of hanging foliage and the smooth, scaly bark are impressive.

In cultivation, Brewer's spruce has not made such large trees, but then it was only introduced in 1897. Give it another 400 years, and who knows what it will make. The tree thrives in drier parts of Britain. Young trees are very slow to adopt the adult weeping foliage, partly because the young foliage is much finer, but also because hanging foliage requires the stem to make height and then develop side branches before the shoots can droop.

Morinda or West Himalayan spruce is superficially similar in the hanging side shoots, and also makes an attractive tree. However, it is not related to Brewer's spruce: its foliage is four sided, more lax on the shoot and green; the cones are much bulkier. It is a native of West Himalaya, preferring moist sites.

The cylindrical crown is curtained by the hanging side shoots and gives the tree its graceful habit.

BARK
Smooth and gray on young trees, developing scaly plates which flake off to reveal brown or purple bark, but remaining rather smooth.

Douglas-fir

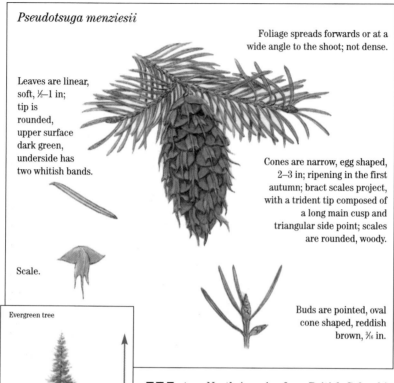

Pseudotsuga menziesii

Foliage spreads forwards or at a wide angle to the shoot; not dense.

Leaves are linear, soft, ½–1 in; tip is rounded, upper surface dark green, underside has two whitish bands.

Cones are narrow, egg shaped, 2–3 in; ripening in the first autumn; bract scales project, with a trident tip composed of a long main cusp and triangular side point; scales are rounded, woody.

Scale.

Evergreen tree

82–197 ft

Buds are pointed, oval cone shaped, reddish brown, ⅜ in.

Western North America from British Columbia through the U.S.A. into central Mexico is the natural range of this species. Covering such a vast area, it shows considerable variation and is usually divided into two subspecies. The typical form, with green foliage and corky bark, is found in northern and coastal parts on the western side of the Rocky Mountains. It grows up to 295 ft and up to 10 ft in diameter. It is a fire-dominant species, regenerating after forest fires and then surviving future ones because of the thick bark. In the absence of fire, it eventually dies and is replaced by shade tolerant species, such as grand fir *Abies grandis* (page 64).

Blue Douglas-fir (subspecies *glauca*) has leaves with a waxy blue covering on the upper surface: a device for restricting water loss. It also has generally smaller and narrower cones with bracts that spread more, and dark gray or blackish, scaly bark, which does not develop the high corky ridges of the green form. It occurs in drier zones on the eastern side of the Rocky Mountains, where it makes a much smaller tree.

Pseudotsuga menziesii makes a majestic tree, used in forestry for its high-quality timber.

BARK
Gray-green and smooth, with blisters of resin on young trees, becoming thick and corky with proud ridges and wide furrows. Reddish brown or gray-brown on old trees.

Pacific silver fir

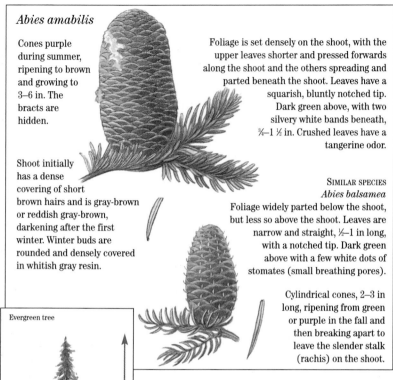

Abies amabilis

Cones purple during summer, ripening to brown and growing to 3–6 in. The bracts are hidden.

Shoot initially has a dense covering of short brown hairs and is gray-brown or reddish gray-brown, darkening after the first winter. Winter buds are rounded and densely covered in whitish gray resin.

Foliage is set densely on the shoot, with the upper leaves shorter and pressed forwards along the shoot and the others spreading and parted beneath the shoot. Leaves have a squarish, bluntly notched tip. Dark green above, with two silvery white bands beneath, ¾–1 ½ in. Crushed leaves have a tangerine odor.

SIMILAR SPECIES
Abies balsamea
Foliage widely parted below the shoot, but less so above the shoot. Leaves are narrow and straight, ½–1 in long, with a notched tip. Dark green above with a few white dots of stomates (small breathing pores).

Cylindrical cones, 2–3 in long, ripening from green or purple in the fall and then breaking apart to leave the slender stalk (rachis) on the shoot.

Evergreen tree

60–200 ft

Pacific silver fir is found from southeastern Alaska to western Oregon, with local populations on mountains in northwestern California. It is a tree of wet or moist conifer forest, and grows both in the coastal fog belt and in inner valleys. It forms pure stands, or grows with other conifers. The Latin name translates as 'beautiful fir', and the dense, luscious foliage makes young trees very attractive. Older trees have an almost blackish appearance against the sky, with short, level branches set on a silvery trunk.

Balsam fir is native from Newfoundland west to Alberta in Canada and in the U.S.A. from Minnesota to New England, with scattered populations in north eastern Iowa and the Virginias. It forms pure stands on swampy sites, but on hillsides grows with white, black and red spruces, aspen and paper birch. The species is shallow rooted, making it likely to be uprooted by strong winds. This is a very resinous tree, with a characteristic scent of balsam. The resin, known as Canada balsam, is used in laboratory work as an optical cement. The tree is not long lived and, like Pacific fir, is vulnerable to forest fires.

The crown of *Abies amabilis* is narrow with short, level branches bearing the dense foliage.

BARK
Thin and silvery white or ash-gray with resin blisters. The bark only becomes scaly at the base in old trees.

Grand fir

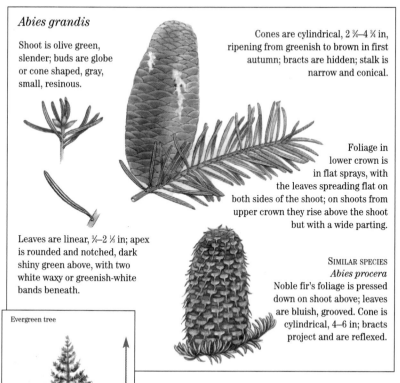

Abies grandis

Shoot is olive green, slender; buds are globe or cone shaped, gray, small, resinous.

Cones are cylindrical, 2 ¾–4 ¼ in, ripening from greenish to brown in first autumn; bracts are hidden; stalk is narrow and conical.

Foliage in lower crown is in flat sprays, with the leaves spreading flat on both sides of the shoot; on shoots from upper crown they rise above the shoot but with a wide parting.

Leaves are linear, ¾–2 ⅛ in; apex is rounded and notched, dark shiny green above, with two white waxy or greenish-white bands beneath.

SIMILAR SPECIES
Abies procera
Noble fir's foliage is pressed down on shoot above; leaves are bluish, grooved. Cone is cylindrical, 4–6 in; bracts project and are reflexed.

Evergreen tree

82–197 ft

Grand fir's native range is from Northern California north to Vancouver Island along the west coast of America and inland into southeastern British Columbia and northern Idaho. It has a rather low-quality timber, partly because it grows so fast. The fastest growing specimens originate from the coastal ranges west of the Cascade Mountains of Oregon and Washington; those originating from east of the Cascades and from Idaho are much slower growing.

In gardens it makes the tallest tree after a hundred years, emerging 33 ft or more above the heads of other trees and suffering from exposure to the wind. It is at its best in sheltered moist sites, where it will retain its foliage down to ground level and can be very attractive.

Noble fir also comes from Oregon and Washington states of the Pacific U.S.A. It has a better quality timber, although in cultivation may form 'drought' cracks in dry years, which show as roughly 3 ft long on the smooth, shiny, silvery-gray bark in the upper part of the trunk. Large cones are produced on young trees. It needs acidic sites, and will not tolerate chalky soils.

Abies grandis is often the tallest tree in its vicinity and so becomes ragged from exposure. But in sheltered sites it retains its foliage down to ground level, as here.

BARK
Smooth, with blisters of resin. Brownish gray on young trees, on old trees cracking into small squares.

White fir

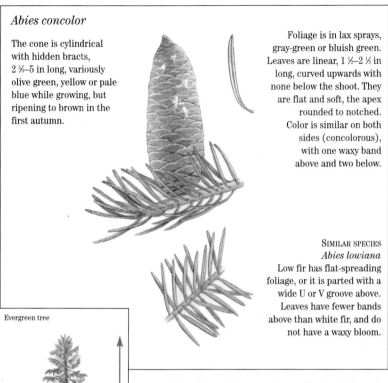

Abies concolor

The cone is cylindrical with hidden bracts, 2 ¾–5 in long, variously olive green, yellow or pale blue while growing, but ripening to brown in the first autumn.

Foliage is in lax sprays, gray-green or bluish green. Leaves are linear, 1 ½–2 ½ in long, curved upwards with none below the shoot. They are flat and soft, the apex rounded to notched. Color is similar on both sides (concolorous), with one waxy band above and two below.

SIMILAR SPECIES
Abies lowiana
Low fir has flat-spreading foliage, or it is parted with a wide U or V groove above. Leaves have fewer bands above than white fir, and do not have a waxy bloom.

Evergreen tree

82–115 ft

White fir originates from Utah, Colorado, Nevada, Arizona, California and New Mexico in southwestern U.S.A. and extends into northern Mexico. It is characterized by sparse foliage which has a waxy bloom on the upper surface of the leaf. In the wild it is an invasive species, regenerating into the stands of other trees. But it can not tolerate fierce forest fires. In cultivation it tolerates drier conditions than the related grand fir, but has no role in forestry. It is sometimes planted as a Christmas tree but mainly it is a park or garden tree, valued for its bright blue foliage.

Low fir is often treated as a variety of white fir. It comes from the Sierra Nevada of California, also Northern California and southwestern Oregon. In cultivation it makes a better tree than white fir, although the foliage is never so blue. The leaves are similarly spaced or lax on the shoot, but the arrangement is much flatter, with fewer lines of stomata or breathing pores. This may be the result of hybridization between white fir and grand fir, and in several respects is intermediate between them.

Abies concolor makes an attractive tree within its bloomed or grayish foliage and will tolerate drier conditions than grand fir.

BARK
Smooth, light to dark gray, with resin blisters on young trees. Thick corky furrows and ridges on old trees.

Western and Eastern hemlock

Tsuga heterophylla

Male flowers are crimson, ⅛–⅜₂ in. They appear in spring.

Cones are egg shaped, ½–1 in, ripening from green to brown in first autumn with around twenty oblong rounded scales.

Foliage is in flat sprays, hanging down at the tips. Leaves are parted above the shoot, linear, ¼–1 in long, tapering to both ends with a bluntly pointed apex. Margins are finely toothed (use a hand lens). Upper surface is mid green, underside has two (or one coalesced) waxy, silver bands.

SIMILAR SPECIES
Tsuga canadensis
Eastern hemlock's foliage always has a line of short leaves lying along the top of the shoot. These show white undersides.

Evergreen tree

82–131 ft

Western hemlock originates from Alaska south to northern California along the Pacific coast of North America, and also occurs inland in south-eastern British Columbia and northern Idaho. It makes a most graceful tree, with dense, green, soft foliage carried on slender shoots hanging down noticeably at the tips. It acquired its common name from the foliage, which has a parsley or hemlock-like scent when crushed. However, it is not poisonous like the true hemlock (which is a herb in the *Umbelliferae* or carrot family). The inner bark is red and has been used to make a form of bread. Western hemlock tolerates a wide range of sites, but particularly likes dry acidic sands. It has an excellent timber, is fast growing, tolerant of shade, but likes shelter.

Eastern hemlock originates in eastern U.S.A. from New England south to Alabama and west to Ontario. It can be distinguished from western hemlock by the line of short upturned leaves along the shoot, which show the silvery under-sides. The buds are smaller, less than ⅒ in. It makes a broader crowned tree, growing mostly in mixed stands with hardwoods, white pine or red spruce.

Graceful in habit and tolerant of dense shade, *Tsuga heterophylla* makes an attractive tree.

BARK
Smooth and purple-brown on young trees, becoming red-brown or gray-brown and developing furrows and scaly ridges.

Scots pine

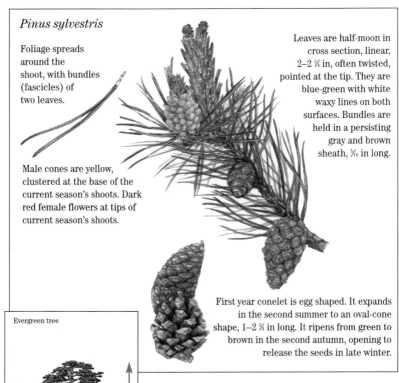

Pinus sylvestris

Foliage spreads around the shoot, with bundles (fascicles) of two leaves.

Leaves are half-moon in cross section, linear, 2–2 ¾ in, often twisted, pointed at the tip. They are blue-green with white waxy lines on both surfaces. Bundles are held in a persisting gray and brown sheath, ⁵⁄₁₆ in long.

Male cones are yellow, clustered at the base of the current season's shoots. Dark red female flowers at tips of current season's shoots.

Evergreen tree

66–98 ft

First year conelet is egg shaped. It expands in the second summer to an oval-cone shape, 1–2 ¾ in long. It ripens from green to brown in the second autumn, opening to release the seeds in late winter.

S cots pine is one of only three conifers native to the British Isles. It has a very wide distribution across Europe and northern Asia as far as northeast China. It is naturalized in North America from New England and southeastern Canada west to Iowa. It is widely planted for shelterbelts, for Christmas trees and as an ornamental for the silvery blue-green foliage. The timber is high quality, known as red deal or yellow deal (the heartwood is reddish, while the outer sapwood is yellow). It is used mainly for sawlogs, but also for veneers and telegraph poles—the modern equivalent of its use for masts and spars of sailing ships in earlier times. In Eurasia, along with birch, Scots pine was the first tree to recolonize the land left bare as the ice retreated after the most recent ice age. It will seed into poor sandy soils, where it can outgrow other trees, but on richer soils it cannot compete with faster-growing broadleaves. The bundles or fascicles of pine tree leaves are actually short shoots. If put together they form a perfect cylinder, whether the tree has two, three or five leaves per fascicle.

Pinus sylvestris makes an attractive tree, with its blue-green foliage and two-colored trunk. It is used in forestry, but also planted in parks and gardens. Young trees are conical but older trees (as here) are rounded and domed at the top.

BARK

On young trees and upper trunk of old trees, red-brown or orange-brown and flaky, abruptly changing to the mature bark, which is purple-gray, fissured with purple-gray ridges shedding small thick scales.

Shore pine

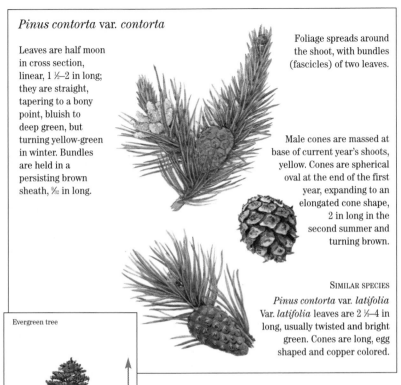

Pinus contorta var. *contorta*

Leaves are half moon in cross section, linear, 1 ½–2 in long; they are straight, tapering to a bony point, bluish to deep green, but turning yellow-green in winter. Bundles are held in a persisting brown sheath, ⁹⁄₃₂ in long.

Foliage spreads around the shoot, with bundles (fascicles) of two leaves.

Male cones are massed at base of current year's shoots, yellow. Cones are spherical oval at the end of the first year, expanding to an elongated cone shape, 2 in long in the second summer and turning brown.

SIMILAR SPECIES

Pinus contorta var. *latifolia*
Var. *latifolia* leaves are 2 ¼–4 in long, usually twisted and bright green. Cones are long, egg shaped and copper colored.

Evergreen tree

49–82 ft

P*inus contorta* is known as both lodgepole pine and shore pine. Shore pine (var. *contorta*) is the form on the Pacific coast of North America from Alaska to Northern California, always within 100 miles of the coast, and frequently on sand dunes just out of reach of the sea. In exposed sites it may only form a shrub, but given better soil and a little shelter, it will make an upright tree, with respectable, if not fast, growth. The timber is satisfactory rather than good. It is tolerant of very poor site conditions and exposure. The long shoots can make either a single node or several nodes: look for the cones which are at the tips of the nodes, and the male cones (or the bare patch they leave) at the base of the shoot above the node. The cones persist on the tree, opening on maturity.

Lodgepole pine (var. *latifolia*) is the form which occurs along the Rocky Mountain chain from the Yukon to Colorado. The foliage is longer and twisted and it makes a tall tree with a narrow crown. This pine is a fire successional species over much of its range, requiring a forest fire to open the cones and scatter the seeds onto a bare, weedfree seedbed.

Pinus contorta can make a large tree when old, with a domed crown, but is more commonly seen in forestry plantings, where the trees are harvested while still with a spiky crown. This photograph shows an example of lodgepole pine intermediate between the two forms. Native Americans used the timber as tent supports.

BARK
Red-brown or yellow-brown on young trees, developing deep fissures and dark scales or plates on old trees.

Austrian or European black pine

Pinus nigra

Leaves are half moon in cross section, linear, 3–5 ½ in long, sharply pointed at the tip, and stiff; they are gray-green, with silvery lines of dots on both surfaces; bundles are held in a persisting dark brown sheath, ⅙–½ in long.

Foliage spreads around the shoot, with bundles (fascicles) of two leaves.

Cones open over winter and fall in the third spring. Cone scales have a blunt ridge.

First year cone is egg shaped, ½ in long, expanding in the second year to an oval cone shape and ripening yellow-brown or brown.

Evergreen tree

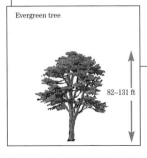

82–131 ft

European black pine is a native of Europe from France and Spain to Turkey, Cyprus and the Ukraine; it is also seen in Morocco and Algeria. It is commonly planted in shelterbelts or as an ornamental and is naturalized in parts of Illinois. It can be divided into two subspecies: ssp. *nigra* includes the trees from southern Austria and central Italy eastwards. This form tends to have denser foliage in more pronounced annual growths. The trees often have several stems, giving characteristic mature habits, and are not much use in forestry. The second subspecies is ssp. *salzmannii* which differs in the longer (4 ¾–7 in), thinner foliage. This form occurs from the Alps into Spain and North Africa, and includes Corsican pine (var. *corsicana*; synonym var. *maritima*) which is found in Corsica, Calabria and Sicily.

Austrian pine makes fast growth on poor sandy soils, but it will also tolerate chalk and limestone soils. It has a reasonable softwood timber, used for sawlogs. It needs full sun for best development, and is well adapted to the harsh Mediterranean climate.

Dense, gray-green foliage on spreading branches gives *Pinus nigra* a distinctive appearance. This is a typical mature ssp. *nigra*.

BARK
Dark brown or greenish-black on young trees, initially smooth, but soon developing deep fissures with broad, scaly ridges.

Colorado pinyon

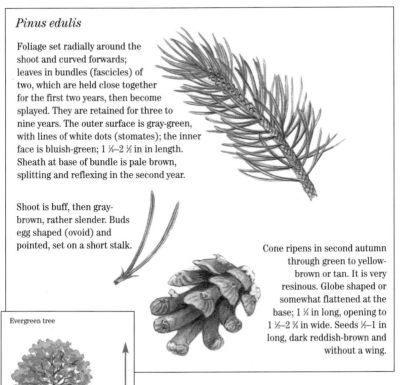

Pinus edulis

Foliage set radially around the shoot and curved forwards; leaves in bundles (fascicles) of two, which are held close together for the first two years, then become splayed. They are retained for three to nine years. The outer surface is gray-green, with lines of white dots (stomates); the inner face is bluish-green; 1 ¼–2 ½ in in length. Sheath at base of bundle is pale brown, splitting and reflexing in the second year.

Shoot is buff, then gray-brown, rather slender. Buds egg shaped (ovoid) and pointed, set on a short stalk.

Cone ripens in second autumn through green to yellow-brown or tan. It is very resinous. Globe shaped or somewhat flattened at the base; 1 ¼ in long, opening to 1 ½–2 ¾ in wide. Seeds ½–1 in long, dark reddish-brown and without a wing.

Evergreen tree

20–50 ft

Pinyon or piñon is found in the area of the southwest U.S.A. between western Texas, Arizona, eastern Utah and Colorado. It is the main tree on the southern rim of the Grand Canyon National Park and grows in open stands on dry rocky slopes or plateaux, either with junipers, or on its own. The climate is dry, with only 12–24 in of rainfall per year, and with the marked temperature contrasts of a semi-desert habitat. Pinyon is well adapted to these conditions, and as in all pines, the needles are designed to conserve moisture.

The species is the dominant tree over a vast swath of territory, and although each specimen usually only carries a few dozen cones each year, the total quantity of seeds or pine kernels produced is enormous. The seeds are oily and very tasty, one of the most palatable of all pine kernels, collected for the gourmet market and for confectionery; once they were a staple food for Native Americans. Much are collected by raiding caches made by animals, rather than by laboriously picking the cones or collecting the nuts from the forest floor. Still, most of the nuts are eaten by wildlife, including jays, turkeys and bears.

Pinus edulis is compact and conical as a young tree, but becomes irregular with a rounded, domed crown as it matures. It mainly makes a small tree, sometimes little more than a shrub.

BARK
Gray and smooth in young trees, developing red-brown furrows and scaly ridges in older trees.

Table-mountain pine

Pinus pungens

Leaves in bundles (fascicles) of two, arranged radially and at first point forwards along the shoot but later spreading, twisted and stiff, ending in a sharp bony point. Gray-green to yellow-green, 1–3 in. Fascicle sheath ½ in, gray and brown, persisting.

Cones egg shaped (ovoid), 2–3 ½ in, ripening to shiny pale brown in the second autumn but usually remaining on the tree for some time in an unopened or partly opened state. Each seed scale has a stout and sharply pointed spine, which is curved forwards. In the open, it fruits when only a few feet in height.

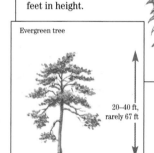

Shoot is multi-nodal, green-brown to brown in first winter, aging to gray or brown. Buds are cylindrical with a rounded-pointed tip, pale brown and thickly resinous.

Evergreen tree

20–40 ft, rarely 67 ft

Table-mountain pine is the only pine restricted to the Appalachian and Piedmont mountain ranges. It occurs from Pennsylvania south to northeastern Georgia, on dry, gravelly and rocky slopes and ridges at up to 4,000 feet. It occurs mainly in association with other pines, but forms pure stands, especially towards the southern end of its distribution. It is a feature of the Great Smoky Mountains and Shenandoah National Parks.

The scientific name *pungens* is the Latin word meaning to prick. It refers to the armature of the cones, which should be handled with care. The Latin word is the root of the English word pungent, meaning sharp, but often used to describe a bad odor—because it pricks the nose. The common name refers to a mountain type, rather than to a specific mountain.

Table-mountain pine makes a rather scrubby tree with a flat-topped and spreading habit. Only rarely, when growing up with other pines, does it reach the right size for commercial timber, but it is used for pulp and firewood. The branches are very tough; hence one of its alternate names, hickory pine.

Pinus pungens usually makes a
low growing tree which is
branched from near the base.

BARK
Dark brown and thick,
becoming furrowed in
scaly plates.

Shortleaf pine

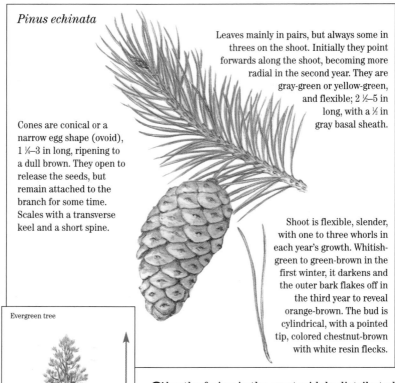

Pinus echinata

Leaves mainly in pairs, but always some in threes on the shoot. Initially they point forwards along the shoot, becoming more radial in the second year. They are gray-green or yellow-green, and flexible; 2 ½–5 in long, with a ½ in gray basal sheath.

Cones are conical or a narrow egg shape (ovoid), 1 ¼–3 in long, ripening to a dull brown. They open to release the seeds, but remain attached to the branch for some time. Scales with a transverse keel and a short spine.

Shoot is flexible, slender, with one to three whorls in each year's growth. Whitish-green to green-brown in the first winter, it darkens and the outer bark flakes off in the third year to reveal orange-brown. The bud is cylindrical, with a pointed tip, colored chestnut-brown with white resin flecks.

Evergreen tree

66–99 ft

Shortleaf pine is the most widely distributed pine in the U.S.A., occurring in 21 states across the Southeast, from New York to eastern Texas, but stopping in northern Florida. It grows naturally on ridges and on sandy loams, or on floodplains, forming pure stands, or mixed with oaks and loblolly pine (page 84).

Shortleaf pine is unusual in its mixture of leaf bundles: it has both two and three-leaved fascicles on the same shoot. In most two-needled pines, it is possible to find the occasional three-needled cluster (similarly, three-needled pines have the occasional bundle of only two needles) but rarely more than two or three per hundred bundles. In shortleaf pine, two and three needles crop up regularly. It is 'short-leaved' in comparison to the other pines of southeastern U.S.A., but in the context of pines as a whole, the leaves are not unduly short. This tree is widely planted across the Southeast as a major source of timber. The wood is useful as construction lumber, making plywood veneers, or for paper-making pulp. It is fast growing and well adapted to dry, sandy sites with full light. Young trees can make new foliage if damaged by fire.

Pinus echinata forms a broad open crown, usually on a long bole.

BARK
Black, or nearly so, in young trees, with reddish-brown scaly plates in old trees.

Pitch pine

Pinus rigida

Leaves in bundles (fascicles) of three, set radially around the shoot like a bottle-brush. Not dense. Stiff and twisted, gray-green, 2 ¾–5 ½ in; persistent, gray-brown fascicle sheath ⁵⁄₁₆ in long.

Cone egg shaped to conical, 1–3 ½ in long. Ripens in the second fall to yellow-brown or gray-brown; opens immediately, but persists. Seed scales with a slender, spreading prickle.

Shoot is rough from the persistent scales at the base of the needle bundles; multi-nodal. Color changes from pale orange-yellow through pale red-brown to brown. Buds are cylindrical, with a conical point, chestnut-brown, thickly resinous.

Evergreen tree

60 ft, rarely to 100 ft

Pitch pine is native to the northeastern states from southern Maine and New York, south to northern Georgia, both in upland areas and on the coastal plain in the northern part of its range. It also extends just across the Canadian border into the extreme south of Quebec and the southeast of Ontario along the northern shore of Lake Ontario. It is found on dry, sandy or gravelly ridges, where it will tolerate drought. It is also on valley bottoms or in swamps. The tree is adapted to survive forest fires and can make new sprouts from the roots or trunk after fire damage. The boles of established trees frequently bear sprouts—few other pines have this characteristic. The New Jersey Pine Barrens are dominated by dwarf shrubs composed of regrowth sprouts following repeated fires. In other habitats, it regenerates after forest fires, but unless fires occur frequently broadleaved trees eventually replace the pine. The timber contains much resin. In colonial times, the tree was tapped for these resins to make turpentine and tar. The knots are especially resinous, and because the resin burns steadily, they can be lit to make torches. The timber is of limited quality, and not available in large sizes.

Pinus rigida has an irregular
domed habit in old trees with
sprout shoots on the bole. Young
trees make a conical or oval shape.

BARK
Dark gray or dark gray-
brown, fissuring into
parallel scaly ridges, often
with sprouts.

83

Loblolly pine

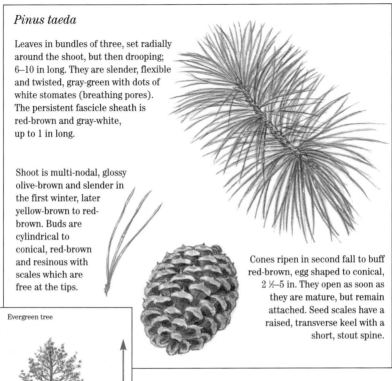

Pinus taeda

Leaves in bundles of three, set radially around the shoot, but then drooping; 6–10 in long. They are slender, flexible and twisted, gray-green with dots of white stomates (breathing pores). The persistent fascicle sheath is red-brown and gray-white, up to 1 in long.

Shoot is multi-nodal, glossy olive-brown and slender in the first winter, later yellow-brown to red-brown. Buds are cylindrical to conical, red-brown and resinous with scales which are free at the tips.

Evergreen tree

100–150 ft

Cones ripen in second fall to buff red-brown, egg shaped to conical, 2 ½–5 in. They open as soon as they are mature, but remain attached. Seed scales have a raised, transverse keel with a short, stout spine.

Loblolly pine is widely distributed in the Southeast, occurring in 15 states in an arc from southern New Jersey south to central Florida and west to central Texas. One meaning of loblolly is a mud puddle. In pre-colonial times it was found on both well-drained hillsides and poorly drained floodplains, but was probably much commoner on wetter sites. However, the forest disturbance caused by European settlement has allowed it to expand onto richer sites. It also goes by the name of oldfield pine, referring to its ability to regenerate into abandoned farmland ahead of other tree species.

The timber is of a fairly good quality, and grows fast in plantations. The tree also produces resins, such as turpentine, and the 'rosin' blocks used by violinists on their bows, which also goes by the quaint name of 'naval stores'. The main use of the resin was once in sailing ships. Modern uses include 'sizing'—the resin fills the pores in paper to make a smooth, glossy paper for fine printing. The resin is collected by steam distillation of wood chips—which are then turned into pulp.

In old age, *Pinus taeda* makes a dense, rounded crown with spreading branches on a stout bole. Younger trees are conical and clothed near to ground level.

BARK
Very dark brown and scaly in young trees, turning blackish-gray with scaly plates and deep fissures showing red-brown inner bark.

Coulter pine

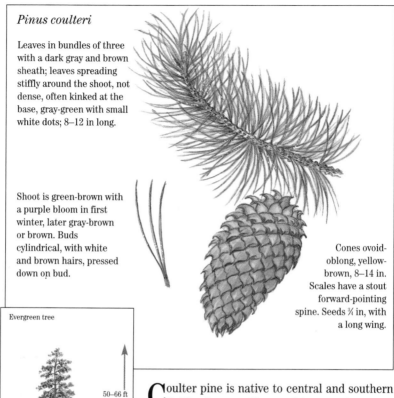

Pinus coulteri

Leaves in bundles of three with a dark gray and brown sheath; leaves spreading stiffly around the shoot, not dense, often kinked at the base, gray-green with small white dots; 8–12 in long.

Shoot is green-brown with a purple bloom in first winter, later gray-brown or brown. Buds cylindrical, with white and brown hairs, pressed down on bud.

Cones ovoid-oblong, yellow-brown, 8–14 in. Scales have a stout forward-pointing spine. Seeds ¾ in, with a long wing.

Evergreen tree

50–66 ft

Coulter pine is native to central and southern California, spreading south into northern Baja California. It has a very characteristic crown due to the horizontally spreading branches, which carry the rather sparse but long gray-green foliage. The leaves are only retained for around three years, so they appear as tufts at the ends of the shoots. It grows on dry rocky slopes and ridges and in chaparral in which it may occur as single scattered trees, but also pure (but open) stands. The cones, weighing up to 4 ½ pounds, are the heaviest of any pine. Their sharp, forward-pointing stout spines, perhaps better described as claws, could cause a serious injury if they fell on someone. Fortunately, the cones generally open on the tree rather than falling intact, releasing the seeds over a period. The seeds are large and like all pine seeds, they are edible, especially if roasted. They were a major food source for Native Americans. Digger pine, *Pinus sabiniana*, is similar in appearance and also occurs in the dry foothills of California. It has blue-green, flexible leaves. The cones are smaller than Coulter pine's, with spreading or reflexed spines and seeds whose wing is only half as long as the seed.

Pinus coulteri has a domed crown with level or ascending branches when mature. Young trees are a broad cone shape.

BARK
Nearly black or dark purple-brown in old trees, but in younger ones gray, with red-brown or brown fissures.

Ponderosa pine

Pinus ponderosa

Leaves are triangular in section, gray-green, 4–8 ½ in long, stiff and linear. They have a bony point. Sheath persistent, brown, ½–¾ in long.

Foliage is arranged radially around the stout gray-brown shoots; leaves are in bundles of three.

Cone is oval shaped in the first year, expanding in second summer when it may be oval cone shaped. It is purple-brown, 2 ¼–6 in long; scales are thin with a reflexed prickle. The cone falls after opening, leaving a ring of scales on the branch.

SIMILAR SPECIES
Pinus jeffreyi
Jeffrey pine's cones are cone to oval cone shaped, rounded at the base when closed, 5–10 in by 2–3 in (closed). Opening to 6 in, they are red brown, falling once ripe, leaving a few scales on the branch.

Jeffrey pine's leaves are gray-green or bluish green, 4 ¾–10 in long. Bundles are held in a persisting sheath ⅝ in long. Leaves are set on stout, waxy bloomed gray-green shoots.

Evergreen tree

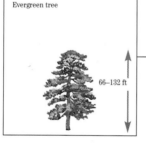

66–132 ft

Ponderosa pine, also known as western yellow pine, is native to western North America from British Columbia to northeastern California, although trees treated as related species or subspecies occur in the eastern flank of the Rocky Mountains and along the Pacific Coast ranges of Washington and California. It grows as a column, with short branches set off the stout trunk and carrying the bold foliage. This is a three-needled pine and, therefore, the leaves have two flat sides and one rounded side, allowing the leaves to come together to form a cylinder. The timber is a good quality and accounts for the alternative name of western yellow pine.

Jeffrey pine occurs from southwestern Oregon through California and western Nevada to Baja California in northern Mexico. It is easily identified by the shoots, with their strong bloom with a waxy layer, and by its cones. Its resin is also different, containing the volatile element heptane, which could be purified to run a car. Jeffrey pine tends to occur on drier and poorer sites than Ponderosa pine. In cultivation it has similarly bold foliage.

Pinus ponderosa makes a majestic
tree as here in a native stand in
Washington east of Mount Rainier,
where it grows with *Abies grandis*
(page 64), *Pinus contorta* (page
72), *Pseudotsuga menziesii* (page
60), *Thuja plicata* (page 30), a
Larix and a *Picea*.

BARK
Dark brown or purple-gray
on young trees, fissuring
and developing broad
flat scaly plates of orange
brown and purple-gray
on old trees.

Monterey pine

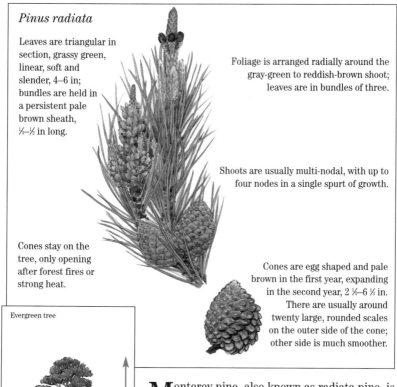

Pinus radiata

Leaves are triangular in section, grassy green, linear, soft and slender, 4–6 in; bundles are held in a persistent pale brown sheath, ⅛–½ in long.

Foliage is arranged radially around the gray-green to reddish-brown shoot; leaves are in bundles of three.

Shoots are usually multi-nodal, with up to four nodes in a single spurt of growth.

Cones stay on the tree, only opening after forest fires or strong heat.

Cones are egg shaped and pale brown in the first year, expanding in the second year, 2 ⅛–6 ⅛ in. There are usually around twenty large, rounded scales on the outer side of the cone; other side is much smoother.

Evergreen tree

Up to 100 ft

Monterey pine, also known as radiata pine, is restricted in the wild to just five sites: three locations on the California coast (the most famous of which is the Monterey Peninsula) and two islands off the coast of Baja California, Mexico. The trees on these two islands differ in having the leaves predominantly in pairs, not threes, and also in their cones, which are often without the score of large rounded scales on the outside. The woody projections on these scales are believed to be a protection against squirrels, as the tree builds up a reserve of seeds in the unopened cones, awaiting a forest fire. The cones may remain on the tree for up to 40 years, but the seeds remain viable for only 20 years. Monterey pine has a reasonable timber, produced very quickly. Thus a tree, which in the wild occupies only a few thousand acres, has been planted over millions of acres in warm temperate parts of the world, especially in New Zealand but also in South Africa, Chile and Spain. In New Zealand a tree is recorded as growing to a height of 197 ft in 37 years, a sharp contrast to the 50–100 ft maximum attained in native stands in California.

Young trees grow fast and have spiky crowns before developing the picturesque rounded domes of old trees.

BARK
Purplish gray on young trees, darkening and becoming deeply furrowed with thick, broad ridges.

Eastern white pine

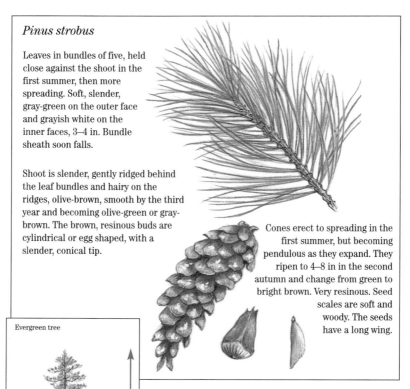

Pinus strobus

Leaves in bundles of five, held close against the shoot in the first summer, then more spreading. Soft, slender, gray-green on the outer face and grayish white on the inner faces, 3–4 in. Bundle sheath soon falls.

Shoot is slender, gently ridged behind the leaf bundles and hairy on the ridges, olive-brown, smooth by the third year and becoming olive-green or gray-brown. The brown, resinous buds are cylindrical or egg shaped, with a slender, conical tip.

Cones erect to spreading in the first summer, but becoming pendulous as they expand. They ripen to 4–8 in in the second autumn and change from green to bright brown. Very resinous. Seed scales are soft and woody. The seeds have a long wing.

Evergreen tree

100–134 ft

Eastern white is characteristic of the old forests of the Northeast, extending in a triangle from Newfoundland west to southeastern Manitoba and south just into northern Georgia. It occurs on well-drained sandy soils, occasionally as a pure stand. However, it is more often found as an emerging tree, growing among and through broadleaved trees. It is a soft pine, so called because of the softness of the cones when compared to the hard pines such as pitch (page 82) and loblolly (page 84), and because of the timber. In hard pines there is a marked difference between the wood formed in the spring—which is composed of water conduction elements—and the summer—which is dense to give strength to the trunk, and so has a distinct, 'two-tone' appearance. In soft pines, this distinction between spring and summer wood is not marked, which makes the wood uniform and more easily worked, especially for carving. In the past, eastern white pine was widely used to make masts for sailing ships, but extensive over-felling occurred during the colonial period. Since then, an introduced fungus, *Cronatium ribicola*, has caused serious loss of trees.

Pinus strobus makes a tall, emergent tree in woodland dominated by broad-leafs.

BARK
Dark gray. In young trees it is smooth, but older trees develop rough bark, with narrow scaly ridges between deep furrows.

Bristlecone pine

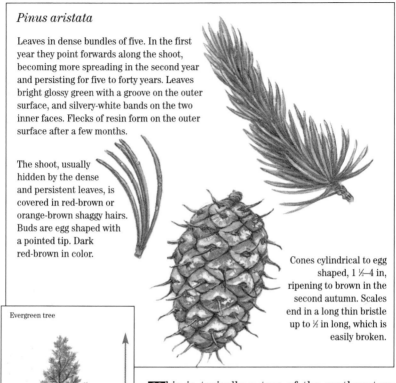

Pinus aristata

Leaves in dense bundles of five. In the first year they point forwards along the shoot, becoming more spreading in the second year and persisting for five to forty years. Leaves bright glossy green with a groove on the outer surface, and silvery-white bands on the two inner faces. Flecks of resin form on the outer surface after a few months.

The shoot, usually hidden by the dense and persistent leaves, is covered in red-brown or orange-brown shaggy hairs. Buds are egg shaped with a pointed tip. Dark red-brown in color.

Cones cylindrical to egg shaped, 1 ½–4 in, ripening to brown in the second autumn. Scales end in a long thin bristle up to ⅕ in long, which is easily broken.

Evergreen tree

20–40 ft

This is typically a tree of the southwestern states: northern Arizona, western Colorado and northern New Mexico. It occurs in alpine and subalpine forests on dry rocky sites, usually in pure stands. In cultivation, it makes a dense, bushy tree. It is named after the slender tips to the seed scales. This is one of the foxtail pines, so called because the dense foliage on the often unbranched smaller boughs look like the tail or brush of a fox. The leaves of bristlecone pine are soon covered in flecks of white resin. Look at an individual leaf closely, and you will see a single groove running along the dorsal face. Beneath this groove is a large resin canal. Some of these canals rupture in the first year, but most in the second summer, spilling their resin, which becomes white as it absorbs moisture. *Pinus aristata* used to be considered the oldest living tree, until it wasdiscovered that specimens from Utah, Nevada and eastern California belong to a related but different species. The oldest trees of bristlecone pine are now believed to be 2,000 years old. This compares with nearly 5,000 years for living specimens of ancient pine, *Pinus longaeva*, from the White Mountains of California.

Pinus aristata makes a bushy tree with a dense crown due to the long, persistent needles.

BARK
Gray to red-brown, becoming shallowly fissured into long, irregular ridges.

Swiss stone pine

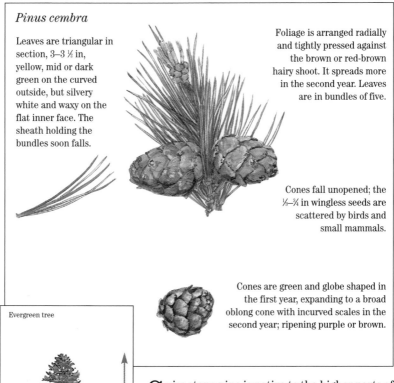

Pinus cembra

Leaves are triangular in section, 3–3 ½ in, yellow, mid or dark green on the curved outside, but silvery white and waxy on the flat inner face. The sheath holding the bundles soon falls.

Foliage is arranged radially and tightly pressed against the brown or red-brown hairy shoot. It spreads more in the second year. Leaves are in bundles of five.

Cones fall unopened; the ½–¾ in wingless seeds are scattered by birds and small mammals.

Cones are green and globe shaped in the first year, expanding to a broad oblong cone with incurved scales in the second year; ripening purple or brown.

Evergreen tree

up to 66 ft

Swiss stone pine is native to the higher parts of the Alps and Carpathian ranges of Central Europe, in subalpine forests. Swiss stone pine is used as a landscape tree in the U.S.A., where it makes a picturesque and very handsome but slow-growing tree which keeps its leaves for 4–5 years. Swiss stone pine is a reference to the large edible seeds. Actually, all pine seeds are edible, but only a few are sufficiently large to be worthwhile.

Swiss stone or Arolla pine belongs to a small group of the soft pines in which the scales do not open to release the seeds. Instead, the whole cone falls intact to the ground where birds and small animals break them open in order to eat or carry off the seeds. Most are eaten sooner or later, but enough are missed to perpetuate the species. It is not an important timber tree due to its subalpine habitat, although the timber is good. It is too slow growing in cultivation to be suitable for forestry plantations. As with most soft pines, the breathing pores or stomata are only found on the flat inner surfaces of the needles and not on the curved outside surface.

Most pines lose their lower
branches as they mature, but given
enough light on an open situation
(as here) *Pinus cembra* can keep
live branches to ground level.

BARK
Dark gray and smooth on
young trees, developing
fissures which expose red-
brown and scaly ridges.

A Key to Broadleaved Trees

'Broadleaved' is a useful enough term. This group of trees generally does have much broader leaves than conifers. They are also known as hardwoods, as opposed to the conifers, which are known as softwoods. Such generalizations don't cover every single case, but most broadleaved trees do have harder or denser timber than the conifers.

The broadleaved trees belong to a larger number of botanical families than the conifers. The 55 genera illustrated as main species in this section of the guide belong to 28 families, compared to 6 families and 20 genera in the conifers.

The order of species in this section is **firstly** by **leaf shape**, with a progression from simple shapes to more complex ones, and only **secondly** by **botanical character**.

Chestnut oak, pages 140-141

Simplest leaf shapes
Pages 102-215 and 282-283
The leaves of these species are either without lobes, or the lobes are extensions of side veins which branch off the central vein.

However, related species are placed together. So, all the oaks follow each other (pages 136-153), even though there are obvious visual differences between, for example, white oak, chestnut oak, northern red oak and live oak.

Joshua tree is placed next to the palms as it is a monocote not a dycote.

White poplar (pages 126-127) has been put in this group, even though its veins place it in the next group, because of its close similarity to aspen (pages 120-121).

Tulip tree or yellow poplar (pages 212-213) is placed next to its close relative, the magnolias, despite having a most unique leaf shape.

Simplest leaf shapes: Gray alder.

of the leaf stalk; they also run to the tips of the lobes. This distinctive leaf shape is called palmate, because the veins start together from the base in the same way that our fingers actually start at the wrist. Normally there are three, five or seven lobes on these leaves, although in *Catalpa* (pages 216-217) and *Paulownia* (pages 218-219) only some leaves have lobes. Hence these two spreads are placed at the beginning of this group; in other words between simplest leaf shapes and palmate leaves. Also see sassafras (pages 188-189) whose leaves may be lobed and unlobed.

Compound leaves
Pages 238-273
Most have pinnately compound leaves: that is, the leaf is divided into a number (almost always an odd number) of leaflets or little leaves, which arise successively along the stalk. Pages 260-269 cover bi-pinnate (or doubly pinnate) leaves in which the leaflets themselves may be divided into leaflets. Honey locust (pages 262-263) may have either pinnate or bi-pinnate leaves on the same branch. Horse chestnut (pages 270-273) is palmately compound, with the leaflets originating as a cluster from one point.

Palmate leaves
Pages 216-237

Palmate leaves: London plane.

In these trees the main leaf veins arise at, or are close to, the top end

Very large leaves
Pages 274-283
These cover the palms, with their enormous leaves.

Compound leaves: walnut.

99

Fruits and seeds
Besides covering leaf shape, this guide also describes fruits and seeds that are likely to help identify a tree.

Rum cherry.

Is it fleshy?
This is the simplest test. Can you stick your thumbnail into the fruit? Pages 164-181, 186-189, 192-193, 196-199, 202-203, 208-211, 214-215, 238-239, 244-249 and 274-281 all have fleshy fruits. Of these, japanese zelkova (pages 164-165), the magnolias (pages 208-211) and hackberry (pages 166-167) have rather thin fleshy layers, which quickly become dry; in butternut, walnut and hickory (pages 244-249) the fleshy layer soon opens to show the hard nut, which may well break your thumbnail. Fruits such as cherry are on pages 170-177; apple and pear are on pages 178-181.

Black oak.

Does the fruit sit in a cup, or is it enclosed by one?
See the beech family (which includes oaks) on pages 136-159.

Is the fruit cluster obviously winged?
The elms (pages 160-163), ashes (pages 240-243) and the tree of heaven (pages 250-251) have seeds either in

Elm.

the middle of a round wing (the elms) or have a wing which tapers around the seed.
    The maples (pages 226-237) have a fruit with the seed sitting very clearly at one end of the wing (and in pairs on the fruit clusters). In hornbeam and hop hornbeam (pages 116-119), the seed sits in a wing-like scale.

Is the fruit like a flattened pea pod?
This is characteristic of the legume family (pages 200-201 and 254-267).

Flattened pod.

Is the fruit or flower a catkin?
Alder or birch (pages 102-115) have catkins; so do poplars and willows (pages 120-135). But also check hornbeam and hop hornbeam and the beech family as the flowers are catkins (pages 116-119 and 136-159), as these also have catkins.

Alder catkin.

Is the fruit a capsule which opens along the side to release seeds?
Catalpa and *Paulownia* (pages 216-219) release winged seeds. Eucalypts (pages 204-207) release small seeds from holes at the top of the fruit. Horse chestnut (pages 270-273) and golden rain tree (pages 268-269) also have capsules.

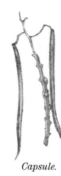

Capsule.

Tulip tree.

If the tree is none of these, check tulip tree (212-213), lindens (pages 182-185), sycamore and plane (pages 220-223) and sweetgum (pages 224-225).

Buds set alternately.

Identifying trees in winter
There are several easy ways to narrow down the possibilities when the leaves have fallen:

Shoots and buds are the most useful characteristics, often narrowing the choices down to at least which genus.
Look first at the arrangement of the buds.

Buds in opposite pairs.

Most trees have the buds set alternately along the shoot, but in olive (pages 196-197), eucalypts (pages 204-207), *Catalpa* (pages 216-217), *Paulownia* (pages 218-219), maples (pages 226-237 and 252-253), ash (pages 240-243) and horse chestnut (pages 270-273) they are in opposite pairs or threes.

Winter silhouette.

This character should always be the first to check because trees with similar leaves, such as maples and sweetgum, ash and rowan, have different bud arrangements.

In winter you will often find leaves from last summer caught up somewhere around the tree. Similarly, look at any fruits remaining on the tree or scattered around it, or debris, perhaps the cup of an acorn.

Willow: single bud scale.

Also look for any special or unusual characteristics, whether in the bark (such as peeling bark of birches, pages 108-115); root suckers growing around the parent tree—such as aspen (pages 120-121) and sassafras (pages 188-189); or buds—willows (pages 128-135) have only a single bud scale. Both alders (pages 102-107) and lindens (pages 182-185) have buds with two bud scales but in alders the buds are set on a short stalk. Only walnut (pages 244-245) and butternut have a chambered pith. These are just a few of the commonest examples.

Gray alder: stalked buds.

Red alder

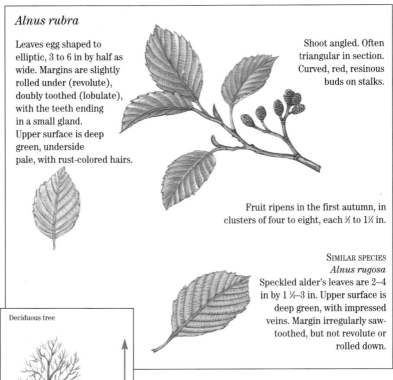

Alnus rubra

Leaves egg shaped to elliptic, 3 to 6 in by half as wide. Margins are slightly rolled under (revolute), doubly toothed (lobulate), with the teeth ending in a small gland. Upper surface is deep green, underside pale, with rust-colored hairs.

Shoot angled. Often triangular in section. Curved, red, resinous buds on stalks.

Fruit ripens in the first autumn, in clusters of four to eight, each ½ to 1¼ in.

SIMILAR SPECIES
Alnus rugosa
Speckled alder's leaves are 2–4 in by 1 ¼–3 in. Upper surface is deep green, with impressed veins. Margin irregularly saw-toothed, but not revolute or rolled down.

Deciduous tree

Up to 100 ft

Red alder is found along the West Coast from southeastern Alaska to central California, but with a discrete population in northern Idaho along the Clearwater River. It is the main broadleaved tree of the region. It grows in damp places, and is the first species to regenerate into landslide sites. Although fast growing, it is not long-lived, and usually gives way to a secondary forest of conifers, which establish under its shelter. Alders form an association with a bacterium, which allows them to fix atmospheric nitrogen and thus make their own nitrogen fertilizer, which is used to enrich poor soils, such as those found on land reclamation sites. The wood is used for pulp and for furniture. It is also useful for firewood, since it does not spit.

Speckled alder is more shrub-like, usually less than 30 ft high. It is found across the continent, but mainly in Canada from the Yukon and eastern British Columbia to Newfoundland. In the U.S.A. it extends south to Iowa, Idaho, and along the Appalachians to West Virginia. The Latin name refers to the impressed veins, which make the upper surface of the leaf uneven or wrinkled.

Alnus rubra makes a fast-growing, upright tree with a single stem and an attractive narrow crown with hanging down branchlets.

BARK
Thin and smooth, nearly white or pale gray. In old trees it breaks into large, flat plates. Inner bark red-brown.

Gray alder

Alnus incana

Leaf is dull green on top, underside is gray and hairy, especially on the nine to twelve pairs of veins; leaf is 2–4 in by 1 ½–2 ½ in; leaf stalk is ⅜–1 in.

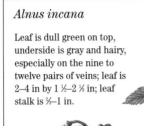

Leaves grow alternately on the shoot, and are oval to egg shaped. Base is wedge shaped to rounded; untoothed except at the base. Apex is pointed. Margin has usually six triangular lobes or coarse teeth with small teeth between.

Shoot is gray or gray-brown, initially with a gray down. Buds are oblong, with two bud scales. Seed is small and narrowly winged.

Catkins, ⅜–1 in long, are exposed over winter, opening in late winter. They are purple-red with yellow pollen and expand to 4 in. Female flowers are red-purple in clusters of three to eight.

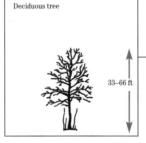

Deciduous tree

33–66 ft

Fruit is an egg shaped woody catkin, ripening to a dark color in the first autumn, ½–1 in long.

G ray alder is native to Europe and the Caucasus but is used as a landscape tree in North America. It is found along streams and rivers, but requires better drainage than common alder and does not grow in water or waterlogged sites. It prefers chalk or limestone sites and will grow, when planted, on drier sites than most other alders. It is unusual in that it sends out suckers from the roots, so mature trees are usually surrounded by a ring of saplings. The tree can be useful in orchards, where it is planted to protect blossoms from late spring frosts: it comes into leaf early, providing shelter, while the narrow crown and light foliage do not compete with the fruit trees for water and nutrients.

Alders have a symbiotic relationship with a group of bacteria, which allows them to fix atmospheric nitrogen into a form that they can use to make proteins. This ability to acquire nitrogen from the air, not just from the soil, allows alders to grow on poor soils, so they are used on land reclamation sites to add nitrogen and leaf litter, and thus to improve the soil.

This tree is typically narrow crowned, with sparse rather than dense branching. The leaves are dull green and do not give good autumn color.

BARK
Dark gray and smooth in young trees, with vertical breathing pores (lenticels). On older trees it is dull gray and fissured.

European alder

Alnus glutinosa

Leaf is shiny deep green on top, initially with sticky glands; underside is pale green with tufts of white hairs in the axils of the veins, of which there are six to eight pairs. Leaves are 1 ½–4 in by 1–3 in; leaf stalk is ½–1 ⅛ in.

Leaves grow alternately on the shoot, and are broadly egg shaped (narrow end attached) to nearly rounded; the base is wedge shaped, the tip is rounded and often notched, the margin is wavy with irregular teeth.

Shoot is initially covered by sticky glands, maturing to gray; buds are oblong, with two scales covered with small gray scales, ⅟₃₂ in, set on a scaly stalk, ³⁄₁₆ in long.

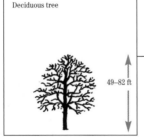

Catkins, ¾–1 in long, are exposed over winter. They open in late winter. At first purple, they shed yellow pollen and expand to 2 ¾ in. Female flowers are egg shaped, red-purple, in clusters of four to five. Fruit is an egg or globe shaped woody catkin, ripening from green to blackish brown; ½–⅝ in long.

Deciduous tree

49–82 ft

Alder is native throughout Europe except for the far north and Iceland, the Faroe Isles, Crete and the Balearic Islands. It is also found in North Africa. In the east, it extends into the Caucasus. In North America, it is naturalized in a band running from New Jersey and Rhode Island west to Minnesota and Iowa, plus in southern Ontario. It is also planted to control erosion or as part of reclamation of mine spoil or sand dunes.

Alder grows mainly along streams and rivers, or in wet flushes where a spring emerges. It can form forests or copses on waterlogged sites, known as alder carrs. It will grow if planted on drier sites, but normally cannot establish as a seedling. The Latin name refers to the clammy glands on the new leaves and shoots, which later dry to black warts. The timber is light and easily worked, hence its historic use for clogs. When fresh it is white, but on exposure to the air it dries to reddish brown. It has little natural durability, except when kept under water. It produces good charcoal, considered the best for gunpowder. Alders will readily coppice if cut down. Old alders on river banks have often been coppiced.

Coppiced *Alnus glutinosa*
in their typical habitat
(see main text, opposite).
The purple cast is caused by the
unexpanded male catkins
(see artwork panel, opposite).

BARK
Purplish brown on young
trees, maturing to gray-
brown and developing
orange or pale fissures.
On old trees it cracks into
small, gray vertical plates.

Paper birch or canoe birch

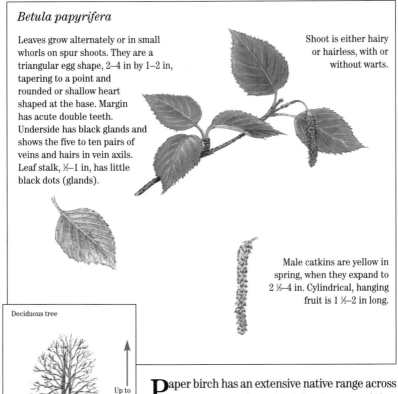

Betula papyrifera

Leaves grow alternately or in small whorls on spur shoots. They are a triangular egg shape, 2–4 in by 1–2 in, tapering to a point and rounded or shallow heart shaped at the base. Margin has acute double teeth. Underside has black glands and shows the five to ten pairs of veins and hairs in vein axils. Leaf stalk, ½–1 in, has little black dots (glands).

Shoot is either hairy or hairless, with or without warts.

Male catkins are yellow in spring, when they expand to 2 ⅛–4 in. Cylindrical, hanging fruit is 1 ½–2 in long.

Deciduous tree

Up to 33–66 ft

Paper birch has an extensive native range across North America from the Atlantic coast of New England and Canada almost to the Pacific Ocean in Alaska, and in the East down the Appalachian Mountains to New York and Pennsylvania. Trees vary across this range, especially in the bark color. Occasional forms exist which are slow to lose the juvenile brown bark. The trunks can grow large enough for the timber mill, and it is also used as an ornamental tree.

As suggested by the name, the most important feature of this tree is the bark. It can be peeled in thin sheets (taking care not to remove the bottom layer, which can damage the tree). Because they contain betulin (the white, waxy constituent of birch bark), the sheets are waterproof, and were used by Native Americans to cover their canoes. The sheets were also used as paper, which is the translation of the Latin name.

Paper birch is generally similar to silver and white birch, and is planted in parks and gardens. The best identifier is the quantity of black dots (resin glands) on the underside of the leaves.

Betula papyrifera is used as an ornamental tree for its attractive bark and golden autumn color.

BARK
Becomes creamy white to chalky white, but often with a pinkish hint; it is brown on young trees.

European white birches

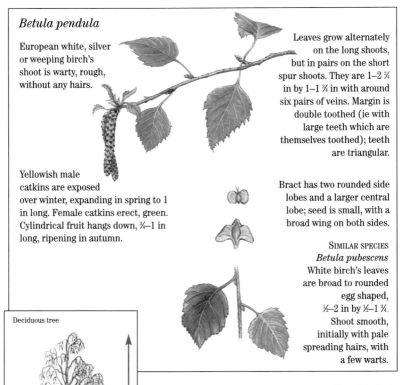

Betula pendula

European white, silver or weeping birch's shoot is warty, rough, without any hairs.

Leaves grow alternately on the long shoots, but in pairs on the short spur shoots. They are 1–2 ¾ in by 1–1 ¾ in with around six pairs of veins. Margin is double toothed (ie with large teeth which are themselves toothed); teeth are triangular.

Yellowish male catkins are exposed over winter, expanding in spring to 1 in long. Female catkins erect, green. Cylindrical fruit hangs down, ¾–1 in long, ripening in autumn.

Bract has two rounded side lobes and a larger central lobe; seed is small, with a broad wing on both sides.

SIMILAR SPECIES
Betula pubescens
White birch's leaves are broad to rounded egg shaped, ½–2 in by ½–1 ¾. Shoot smooth, initially with pale spreading hairs, with a few warts.

Deciduous tree

33–52 ft

European white birch, also called silver birch, is native to Europe from Spain and Britain east into northern Asia. It is widely planted for the silvery white trunk and pendulous foliage and has become naturalized in places, especially in the Northeast and in the West in parts of Washington and British Columbia. It grows on light well-drained soils, making a fast-growing small tree which rarely lives for more than 50 years. The wood is light and used to make birch plywood. In spring the sap contains sugars and can be tapped to make beer or wine. White birch *Betula pubescens* has a similar range in Europe to silver birch but also occurs in Iceland and Greenland, thus making it a North American tree. It is superficially similar, differing in the singly toothed leaves. The leaves and shoots are also hairy (without warts).Gray birch, *Betula populifolia*, is even closer to silver birch, differing primarily in the long drawn-out point to the leaves. It is native to the Northeast, extending from Cape Breton Island to New Jersey and west to Indiana and southern Ontario. It is a short-lived pioneer species, growing for a few decades but giving way to slower-growing, larger and longer-lived trees.

Betula pendula makes a graceful tree with a light delicate crown, usually turning a beautiful yellow in autumn.

BARK
Silvery white in the upper crown. On old trees it fissures to give thick, corky ridges at the base.

Yellow birch

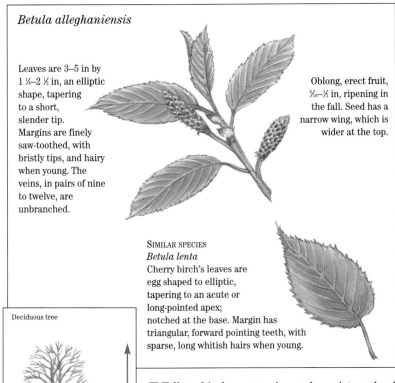

Betula alleghaniensis

Leaves are 3–5 in by 1 ¼–2 ½ in, an elliptic shape, tapering to a short, slender tip. Margins are finely saw-toothed, with bristly tips, and hairy when young. The veins, in pairs of nine to twelve, are unbranched.

Oblong, erect fruit, ⁵⁄₁₆–½ in, ripening in the fall. Seed has a narrow wing, which is wider at the top.

SIMILAR SPECIES
Betula lenta
Cherry birch's leaves are egg shaped to elliptic, tapering to an acute or long-pointed apex; notched at the base. Margin has triangular, forward pointing teeth, with sparse, long whitish hairs when young.

Deciduous tree

33–66 ft

Yellow birch occurs in cool, moist, upland regions from Newfoundland west to Manitoba and Iowa, and south to Georgia. It grows with other broadleaved trees, or with conifers. An important timber tree, it provides about three quarters of all birch lumber. The twigs are covered by dense, long hairs when new, but mature to shiny yellow-brown or dark brown. If the bark is removed, there is a strong smell of methyl salicylate or oil of wintergreen, used in antiseptic creams.

Cherry or black birch also has the oil of wintergreen scent. It is found in the East from Maine and southern Ontario to Alabama and Ohio, mainly along the Appalachian Mountain range. It is closely related to yellow birch, but its genetic make-up is different: it is a diploid, with two sets of chromosomes, unlike yellow birch, which has six sets. The main differences are in the shoots, bark and fruits. The shoots are almost hairless, even when young. The fruits are similarly not hairy, and are longer, up to 1–1 ½ in. The wing around the seeds is more even in width, not broader near the tip. Birches bleed profusely if cut in early spring; the sap can be fermented to make birch beer.

Betula alleghaniensis develops a broad, rounded crown with drooping branches in old trees, giving a spectacular autumn display of bright yellow.

BARK
Yellowish-gray or silvery gray, peeling into small, papery rolls.

113

River birch

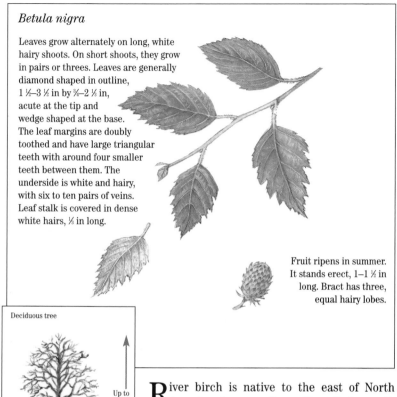

Betula nigra

Leaves grow alternately on long, white hairy shoots. On short shoots, they grow in pairs or threes. Leaves are generally diamond shaped in outline, 1 ½–3 ½ in by ¾–2 ½ in, acute at the tip and wedge shaped at the base. The leaf margins are doubly toothed and have large triangular teeth with around four smaller teeth between them. The underside is white and hairy, with six to ten pairs of veins. Leaf stalk is covered in dense white hairs, ⅛ in long.

Fruit ripens in summer. It stands erect, 1–1 ½ in long. Bract has three, equal hairy lobes.

Deciduous tree

Up to 33–49 ft

River birch is native to the east of North America from southern New York, south along the Atlantic Coast and Gulf Coast to Texas and north to Wisconsin: the most southerly of the American birch species. It is a tree of wet places, restricted through most of its range to boggy riverside sites which flood at periods of high water. In cultivation it will happily grow on most soils. However, the ripening of the fruit in summer is related to its natural habitat: the water level is lowest during the summer and, therefore, the seeds are produced at this time, so they can germinate in the damp soil before being inundated.

River birch is also known as black birch (and sometimes, confusingly, as red birch). This is a reference to the bark of very old trees which becomes black and flakes in small scales. However, most trees in cultivation are much younger and only show the buff or orange-whitish bark, which has a betulin content and flakes attractively. The erect fruits, the white, hairy diamond-shaped leaves and the shoots, which are covered in dense white hairs when young, help to distinguish river birch from other birches.

Betula nigra makes an attractive ornamental tree. Old trees have an unusual bark, becoming thick and shaggy but in young trees (see right) it is shiny pink-brown or silvery gray. It is often multi-stemmed at or near the base.

BARK
Buff pink or orange on young trees, developing large peeling flakes. On old trees, it becomes black or reddish and develops peeling flakes.

American hornbeam

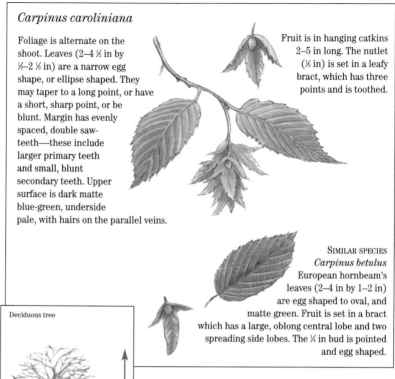

Carpinus caroliniana

Foliage is alternate on the shoot. Leaves (2–4 ½ in by ½–2 ½ in) are a narrow egg shape, or ellipse shaped. They may taper to a long point, or have a short, sharp point, or be blunt. Margin has evenly spaced, double saw-teeth—these include larger primary teeth and small, blunt secondary teeth. Upper surface is dark matte blue-green, underside pale, with hairs on the parallel veins.

Fruit is in hanging catkins 2–5 in long. The nutlet (⅛ in) is set in a leafy bract, which has three points and is toothed.

SIMILAR SPECIES
Carpinus betulus
European hornbeam's leaves (2–4 in by 1–2 in) are egg shaped to oval, and matte green. Fruit is set in a bract which has a large, oblong central lobe and two spreading side lobes. The ¼ in bud is pointed and egg shaped.

Deciduous tree

Up to 40 ft

American hornbeam occurs in two distinctive phases or forms. The typical subspecies *caroliniana* is found mainly along the Atlantic and Gulf coastal plains from New Jersey to eastern Texas and north as far as southern Missouri and southern Illinois. This makes a smallish tree, usually less than 30 ft in height.

The subspecies *virginiana* is found farther north, especially in the Appalachians and interior forests in the Northeast. This subspecies has larger leaves than the subspecies *caroliniana*, 3–5 in, and taper to a drawn-out tip, with secondary teeth which are nearly as large as the primary teeth. The leaves have conspicuous dark glands on the underside, not seen on *caroliniana*. It makes a taller tree, reaching 40 ft. The two forms hybridize where they meet.

European hornbeam, *Carpinus betulus*, is more common in parks and gardens than American hornbeam, and it makes a larger tree, reaching 80 ft. It is most easily separated (especially from *virginiana*) when in fruit. Hornbeams have very hard, tough wood—in fact hornbeam derives from the Anglo-Saxon words horn, meaning hard, and beam, meaning tree.

Carpinus caroliniana makes a
spreading, often bushy tree with a
rounded, spreading crown.

BARK
Smooth, gray and often
fluted. Looks rather like
beech's bark.

American hop hornbeam

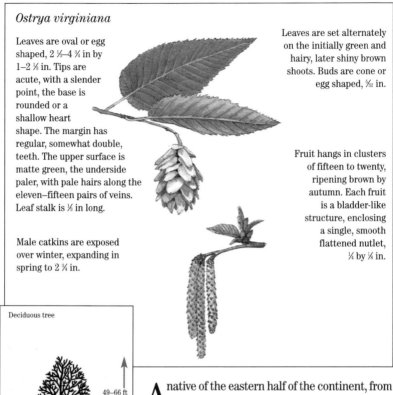

Ostrya virginiana

Leaves are oval or egg shaped, 2 ⅖–4 ¾ in by 1–2 ⅛ in. Tips are acute, with a slender point, the base is rounded or a shallow heart shape. The margin has regular, somewhat double, teeth. The upper surface is matte green, the underside paler, with pale hairs along the eleven–fifteen pairs of veins. Leaf stalk is ⅙ in long.

Male catkins are exposed over winter, expanding in spring to 2 ¾ in.

Leaves are set alternately on the initially green and hairy, later shiny brown shoots. Buds are cone or egg shaped, ⁵⁄₃₂ in.

Fruit hangs in clusters of fifteen to twenty, ripening brown by autumn. Each fruit is a bladder-like structure, enclosing a single, smooth flattened nutlet, ¼ by ⅛ in.

Deciduous tree

49–66 ft

A native of the eastern half of the continent, from southern Manitoba south to eastern Texas and east to the coast from Florida to Nova Scotia, hop hornbeam occurs as an understory tree in moist soils on upland hardwood sites. The 'hop' in the common name refers to the similarity of the fruit to that of the hop used to flavor beer, although it cannot be used to such good effect, and ironwood, its alternate name, to the hardness of the wood. The seeds are completely enclosed in their bladder-like shell, and the generic name *Ostrya* is from the Greek for a shell. The tree is closely related to the hornbeams, sharing similar foliage and a timber of similar hardness, put to similar uses. *Ostrya* can be separated from the hornbeams when in fruit by the bladder and, when not in fruit, by the male catkins, exposed from when they are formed in the summer until they expand in the spring. On hornbeams, they are enclosed within the buds. The bark is very different too; perhaps the easiest identifier. Hop hornbeam makes an attractive tree, flourishing on all well-drained soils. It is particularly effective when the male catkins expand in the spring and when the foliage turns yellow in autumn.

Ostrya virginiana looks dense and leafy in early summer, as this photograph shows. It has good autumn color and is attractive in early spring when the catkins expand.

BARK
Becomes rough (almost shaggy) and fissured early in life and develops coarse scaly plates which reveal an orange-brown beneath.

Quaking aspen

Populus tremuloides

Leaves are round to egg shaped (broad end attached) in outline, ½–3 in long and wide. Tip is rounded, base is rounded or a shallow heart shape. Margin is finely saw-toothed. Upper surface is bluish green, underside bloomed or pale green. Young leaves have white hairs and are usually copper colored. Leaf stalk is 1½–3 in, rounded near the base, but flattened near the blade, allowing it to move in the slightest breeze.

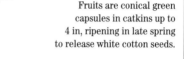

Leaves are set alternately along the shoots, which are shiny olive green, later brown. Buds are oval to cone-shaped, shiny brown, ¼ in.

Fruits are conical green capsules in catkins up to 4 in, ripening in late spring to release white cotton seeds.

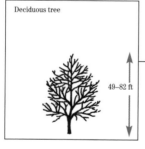

Male flowers are on shoots which are ridged behind the egg shaped buds. They open in spring and are 2–4 in long.

Deciduous tree

49–82 ft

Quaking aspen is native across Canada to Alaska. In the East it extends south into Virginia. In the West, it extends even farther south along the Rocky Mountains into northern Mexico. It is restricted to moist sites, but once established can reproduce by suckers from the root system, and a single plant spreads over a large area. Aspen also reproduces by seed, which is light and blown by the wind. As with most poplars, there are male and female trees.

The shape of the leaf stalk or petiole allows the leaves to move in the slightest breeze, causing both movement and noise as the stiff leaves rattle together, and explains the common name of 'quaking aspen'. The timber is soft, burning slowly without spitting, and is used to make matches.

Bigtoothed aspen, *Populus grandidentata*, is found in north and eastern America from Manitoba to Newfoundland and south to Virginia and Minnesota. It differs in the broad egg shaped leaves, which bear large, coarse and curved teeth. It is a pioneer species, regenerating after logging or fire damage. It is short-lived, though, and succeeded by conifers which regenerate in its shelter.

Populus tremuloides makes a tree with a column shaped crown and is often surrounded by root suckers. Its autumn color can be stunning—as seen here.

BARK
Smooth and grayish green on young trees, with prominent breathing pores (lenticels). It develops shallow ridges at the base of old trees.

Lombardy poplar

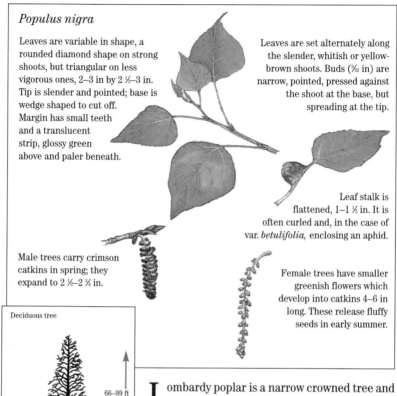

Populus nigra

Leaves are variable in shape, a rounded diamond shape on strong shoots, but triangular on less vigorous ones, 2–3 in by 2 ½–3 in. Tip is slender and pointed; base is wedge shaped to cut off. Margin has small teeth and a translucent strip, glossy green above and paler beneath.

Leaves are set alternately along the slender, whitish or yellow-brown shoots. Buds (⅜₂ in) are narrow, pointed, pressed against the shoot at the base, but spreading at the tip.

Leaf stalk is flattened, 1–1 ½ in. It is often curled and, in the case of var. *betulifolia,* enclosing an aphid.

Male trees carry crimson catkins in spring; they expand to 2 ¼–2 ¾ in.

Female trees have smaller greenish flowers which develop into catkins 4–6 in long. These release fluffy seeds in early summer.

Deciduous tree

66–99 ft

Lombardy poplar is a narrow crowned tree and is planted in shelterbelts throughout the drier parts of North America, especially in the Great Basin. It is a male form of the European black poplar. The parent species is found throughout Europe, east into central Asia and south into North Africa, and was introduced to North America in colonial times. Lombardy poplar is believed to have been selected from the Lombard district of northern Italy, but may have been introduced there by travelers such as Marco Polo nearly a thousand years ago.

Closely related to Lombardy poplar is the Eastern cottonwood, *Populus deltoides.* This is native to a broad chunk of North America from Texas northwest to southern Alberta and east to New Hampshire. It just gets into Florida in the western end of the panhandle. It differs in the leaves having hairs on the margin and in the fruits on female trees opening along three or four valves (only two in female trees of Lombardy poplar). The name refers to the cotton which is attached to the small seeds, and blows everywhere. It thrives on wet valley bottoms, or stream sides, and is often mixed with willows.

Populus nigra is the most commonly seen form of black poplar, often planted away from the damp riverside habits favored by the species. It makes a tall tree, up to 100 ft, with a massive trunk and head of branches.

BARK
Gray-brown, developing deep fissures with short broad ridges; often with burrs.

Black cottonwood

Populus trichocarpa

Leaves are long egg shaped to oblong, 2 ¾–6 in by 2–4 in. The apex tapers to a slender point; base is rounded or a shallow heart shape.

Leaves are set alternately along the shoots. These are slightly angled and hairy when young, but become round and hairless as they mature to shiny reddish brown. Buds are narrow, up to 1 in long, pointed; they are reddish brown, but give out yellow resin with a balsam scent.

The margin has shallow, wavy teeth without a translucent strip. Upper surface is dark, shiny green. Underside is white or yellowish white with an oily texture and net veining. Leaf stalk is round in section.

Fruiting catkins hang down. Capsules open in three places to release masses of fluffy seeds.

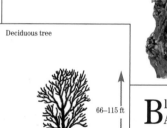

SIMILAR SPECIES
Populus candicans
Balm of Gilead's leaf is egg shaped (broad end attached) with a hairy margin. Trunk is disfigured by cankers.

Deciduous tree

66–115 ft

Black cottonwood is native to western North America from Alaska south to Baja California of northern Mexico and inland to Alberta, Montana and South Dakota. It forms a neat column shaped, crowned tree with a dense, leafy habit and turns yellow in autumn. It is grown as a specimen, and, like other poplars, likes damp sites. It has the light, soft timber typical of poplars.

The common name cottonwood refers to the cotton (strands of cellulose) which are attached to the small seeds and helps them to disperse in the wind. Only female poplars produce seeds, and are much unloved by those who hang out their washing in June: the seeds stick to damp clothes. Another common name for the tree is western balsam poplar: its new foliage has a strong balsam scent. The second word in the Latin name translates as 'hairy fruit'.

Balm of Gilead is a female tree of uncertain origin. It may be a form of the eastern balsam poplar (from eastern North America), or a hybrid of this with *Populus deltoides*. It makes a smaller-growing tree with beautiful balsam-scented foliage. It is often grown as the clone 'Aurora'.

Populus trichocarpa forms a column shaped crown and often suckers at the base.

BARK
Gray-green or yellowish gray and smooth, but on older trees turns grayer and fissures.

White poplar

Populus alba

Shoots are a vivid white and woolly when young; but the hairs are soon lost, revealing green, which matures to brown beneath. Leaves and buds alternate. Buds are egg shaped and pointed, orange-brown with white hairs.

Leaves (2⅓–4¾ in) are always silver white and woolly when young. The wool soon rubs off the upper surface, leaving it a shiny, dark green, but remains grayish white on the underside. Shape is variable, with three to five triangular lobes with a few teeth. Base is rounded or a shallow heart shape. Margin has no translucent strip, size from 2⅓–4¾ in. Leaf stalk is slightly flattened, woolly.

Male catkins appear in spring before the leaves. They are crimson, with gray wool, and expand to 3 in.

Female catkins are green, expanding as the fruit ripens to 3–4 in.

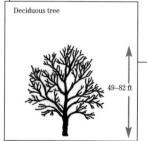

SIMILAR SPECIES
Populus canescens
Leaves of gray poplar are gray and hairy beneath when young, toothed but not lobed, except on the most vigorous shoots.

Deciduous tree

49–82 ft

White poplar, also known as abele, is native to Europe from Portugal and Spain in the west, north through central France and Germany, and from there east into Central Asia; it is also native to coastal North Africa. It has been widely planted outside these areas, including North America, for its attractive, silvery foliage. As it suckers from the roots, plantings soon form clumps and appear to present natural stands. The natural habitat is fertile, well-drained but damp soils in full sun. Like other poplars, it does not tolerate shade, but, unlike most, it will not tolerate waterlogged sites. The timber is soft and white.

Gray poplar is a natural hybrid between white poplar and European aspen, intermediate between the two parent species, but with hybrid vigor. It occurs where the two species grow together, but is also widely planted as a specimen tree. As with both parents, it suckers profusely and soon establishes a grove of saplings. The leaves are initially hairy, as in white poplar, but gray rather than vivid silver. Their shape, especially on the weaker shoots, is rounded as in aspen; only the most vigorous shoots produce strongly lobed leaves.

The rounded, domed crown of *Populus alba* is particularly attractive when the leaves are moved by the wind to reveal the vivid silver-white undersides. Illustrated here is an old tree growing beside the Yarlung Tsangpo in southeast Tibet.

BARK
Gray-green or creamy white, smooth on young trees, with small black pits. It becomes black, cracked and furrowed at the base of old trees.

127

Black willow

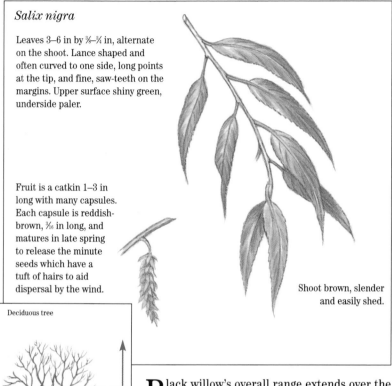

Salix nigra

Leaves 3–6 in by ⅜–¾ in, alternate on the shoot. Lance shaped and often curved to one side, long points at the tip, and fine, saw-teeth on the margins. Upper surface shiny green, underside paler.

Fruit is a catkin 1–3 in long with many capsules. Each capsule is reddish-brown, ³⁄₁₆ in long, and matures in late spring to release the minute seeds which have a tuft of hairs to aid dispersal by the wind.

Shoot brown, slender and easily shed.

Deciduous tree

60–100 ft

Black willow's overall range extends over the entire eastern half of the continent, although only just into Canada. However, in the western half of the continent it is irregular, with scattered populations from western Texas to northern California and south just into Mexico. These trees tend to have smaller leaves and are a duller green than those seen in the East. Black willow prefers wet soils, such as are found along streams or on lake shores, or in areas prone to seasonal flooding. It is often in company with cottonwoods. The preference for damp sites is explained mainly by the way the minute seeds germinate. They contain almost no food reserves, so must germinate quickly to continue their growth away from the 'parent'. The quantity of seeds produced is vast, and most fall on stony or dry ground, but some land on suitable sites. Once the seed has germinated and made a few days growth, it can survive on a dryish site—so planted trees will flourish where the tree would not normally establish itself in the wild. This is the largest of the native willows. It is used for pulp, and it is a source of light, easily worked timber.

Salix nigra (in the foreground) is often seen as three or four stems, which eventually make a broad, open crown. This is a young tree.

BARK
Dark brown to almost black, deeply fissured into scaly forked ridges and flaking, but young trees have pinkish-gray bark.

White willow

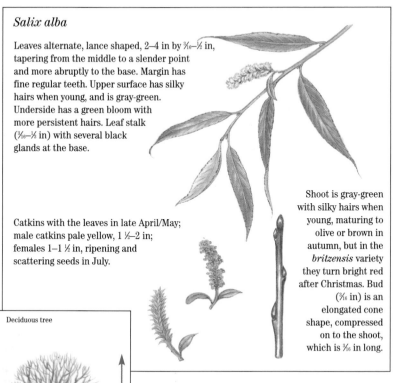

Salix alba

Leaves alternate, lance shaped, 2–4 in by ³⁄₁₆–½ in, tapering from the middle to a slender point and more abruptly to the base. Margin has fine regular teeth. Upper surface has silky hairs when young, and is gray-green. Underside has a green bloom with more persistent hairs. Leaf stalk (³⁄₁₆–⅓ in) with several black glands at the base.

Catkins with the leaves in late April/May; male catkins pale yellow, 1 ½–2 in; females 1–1 ½ in, ripening and scattering seeds in July.

Shoot is gray-green with silky hairs when young, maturing to olive or brown in autumn, but in the *britzensis* variety they turn bright red after Christmas. Bud (³⁄₁₆ in) is an elongated cone shape, compressed on to the shoot, which is ³⁄₁₆ in long.

Deciduous tree

33–99 ft

This species is native from southern England across Europe and into Central Asia. In North America it was planted in colonial times and has become naturalized in southeast Canada and eastern U.S.A.. It thrives on damp sites that may be flooded from time to time; or it grows beside streams and rivers with other species that like a damp situation. However, it also grows happily on less damp sites if planted, though it won't regenerate naturally on these sites. The timber is soft and light, yet also springy and withstands shocks. It is also used as an ornamental tree and for shelterbelts. It can be propagated from large unrooted cuttings or 'sets'. The quintessentially English game of cricket (although played with more success in the Caribbean, Australia and the Indian subcontinent!) requires a bat made from the wood of this species.

Two other varieties are *britzensis*, whose red twigs lighten up the countryside after Christmas—it is particularly effective in February sun and can be grown as a coppiced shrub; and *argentea*, which has many more silky hairs on the leaves, making a silvery-gray tree.

Salix alba is commonly found growing along river banks, where it forms an attractive tree with its dense, leafy crown. This is conical in young trees and rounded or domed in old ones.

BARK
Gray-brown, becoming deeply fissured and ridged.

Crack willow

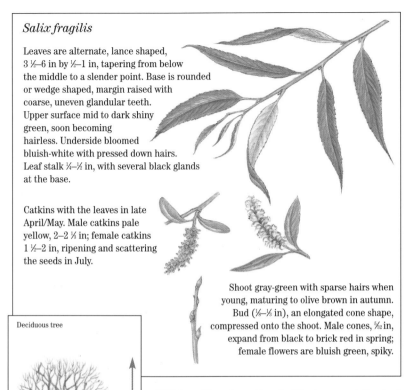

Salix fragilis

Leaves are alternate, lance shaped, 3 ½–6 in by ½–1 in, tapering from below the middle to a slender point. Base is rounded or wedge shaped, margin raised with coarse, uneven glandular teeth. Upper surface mid to dark shiny green, soon becoming hairless. Underside bloomed bluish-white with pressed down hairs. Leaf stalk ¼–½ in, with several black glands at the base.

Catkins with the leaves in late April/May. Male catkins pale yellow, 2–2 ⅛ in; female catkins 1 ½–2 in, ripening and scattering the seeds in July.

Shoot gray-green with sparse hairs when young, maturing to olive brown in autumn. Bud (⅛–⅓ in), an elongated cone shape, compressed onto the shoot. Male cones, ⁵⁄₃₂ in, expand from black to brick red in spring; female flowers are bluish green, spiky.

Deciduous tree

33–66 ft

This willow is native to Western and Central Europe from Norway and Britain south to Spain and across to Romania. In North America it is naturalized from Newfoundland west to South Dakota and south to Kansas and Virginia. It makes a smaller tree than the closely related white willow (page 130) from which it can be distinguished by the much less hairy and generally larger leaves which are glossy above and taper from below the middle.

The name crack willow (and the scientific name *fragilis*, which translates as fragile) refer to the way in which second-year twigs will snap with a clear but staggered break on only a very light backward pressure. Twigs older than two years do not snap easily, neither do the current year's twigs until they have ripened. The snapped twigs will root if they land on suitably damp soil, and establish a forest of saplings. Crack and white willows are frequently grown as pollards along river banks. These are formed by cutting the trunk off at 10 ft. The resulting new growths (out of reach of horses and cattle) are harvested for small timber or cut for winter fodder.

The crown of *Salix fragilis* is rounded (as shown here) if a tree has grown in the open. Young trees are spiky and conical; older ones are more ragged because they lose branches in strong winds.

BARK
Gray, scaly when young and developing coarse, deep fissures with thick ridges when mature.

Weeping willow

Salix sepulcralis 'Chrysocoma'

Leaves are alternate on the shoot, narrow and lance shaped, 2 ¾–5 in by ½ in, tapering gently to the pointed tip and wedge shaped at the base. Margins have small teeth. Upper surface is matte to shiny green with some silky hairs, underside bluish green with a raised silky haired midrib. Leaf stalk (to ⅕ in) has a few black glands.

Shoot hangs down, green and hairy at first, but maturing to golden-green by mid winter. Buds (³⁄₁₆ in) are a narrow egg shape, pressed against shoot.

Deciduous tree

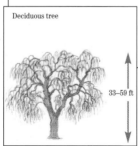

33–59 ft

Weeping willow is a hybrid of white willow (page 130) and the Chinese weeping willow, *Salix babylonica* (see below). The commonest form is the cultivar 'Chrysocoma' which has a golden-twigged form of white willow as one parent. With its golden twigs and vigorous weeping habit, this has supplanted other forms of weeping willow. Like most willows, 'Chrysocoma' roots readily from cuttings and is propagated commercially from hardwood cuttings taken in late winter and stuck into the ground. However, a twig broken off in mid winter will root if placed in water on a windowsill, with the white roots erupting from the stem just beneath the water's surface after a week or so.

Salix babylonica, a Chinese species, is the tree illustrated on the 'willow' pattern of china. It was given the scientific name *babylonica* because it was originally identified as the willow in Psalm 137, verse 2. However, this is now believed to be an incorrect translation, as the trees referred to in the psalm were, in fact, poplars. *Salix babylonica* can be distinguished by the green or brownish-green shoots and the long, slender twisted tip of the leaves.

Salix sepulcralis 'Chrysocoma' is very graceful when growing beside a lake or river with its branches hanging over the water and reflected in it.

BARK
Golden-green and smooth on young trees. After several years it turns brown and develops coarse ridges and fissures.

135

White oak

Quercus alba

Leaves (4–10 in by 2–4 in) alternate on the shoot, but clustered towards the end. Ellipse shaped, with five to nine moderate to deep lobes which are often narrowed and rounded at the tips and separated by deep sinuses (indentations) extending between ⅛ and ⅞ths of the way to the midrib. Upper surface light green, at first with erect, whitish or greenish hairs. Underside light gray-green, matte or glossy.

Acorn matures in the first autumn, after pollination. Egg shaped (ovate), ¾–1 in long, the bottom quarter enclosed by a shallow, light gray, hairy cup.

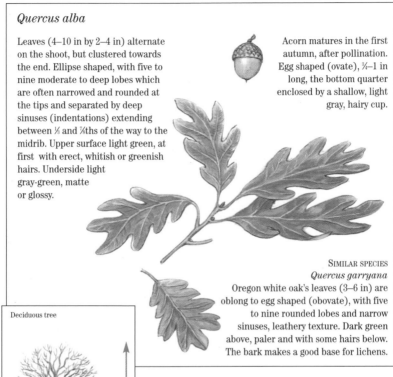

SIMILAR SPECIES
Quercus garryana
Oregon white oak's leaves (3–6 in) are oblong to egg shaped (obovate), with five to nine rounded lobes and narrow sinuses, leathery texture. Dark green above, paler and with some hairs below. The bark makes a good base for lichens.

Deciduous tree

Up to 80 ft

White oak occurs across the eastern half of the country from eastern Texas to Georgia and north to Maine and west to Minnesota, extending into northern Florida in the south and southern Ontario and just into Quebec. It grows mostly on welldrained, moist to dry soils, less often on rocky slopes with thin soil, or on barren land. Long lived, it is also rather slow growing. The lumber is hard and heavy, with a strong, light brown heartwood. Today it is used in furniture-making; in the past it was a wood of choice for barrels. The alternative name, stave oak, derives from this use. The timber was also used in wooden sailing ships. The white oaks are a large group (fifty-one in North America), characterized by the acorn ripening in the first autumn.

Oregon white oak is found in the West, extending from southern British Columbia to California. It mainly occurs along the coastal ranges, but also grows in the Sierra Nevada and is the only oak in Washington and British Columbia. Oregon white oak forests are found on the margins of redwood groves or in oak forests on moist to dry sites.

Quercus alba forms a rounded crown, with stout, wide-spreading branches.

BARK
Light ash gray, with shallow fissures and broad, scaly, loose plates.

English or pedunculate oak

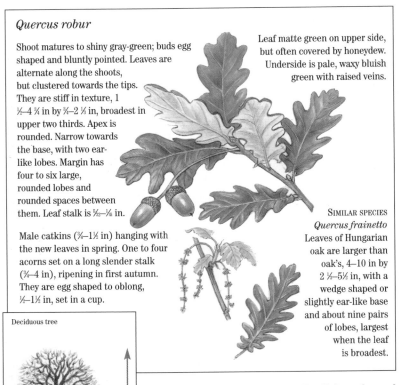

Quercus robur

Shoot matures to shiny gray-green; buds egg shaped and bluntly pointed. Leaves are alternate along the shoots, but clustered towards the tips. They are stiff in texture, 1 ½–4 ¾ in by ¾–2 ⅛ in, broadest in upper two thirds. Apex is rounded. Narrow towards the base, with two ear-like lobes. Margin has four to six large, rounded lobes and rounded spaces between them. Leaf stalk is ⅒–¼ in.

Male catkins (¾–1½ in) hanging with the new leaves in spring. One to four acorns set on a long slender stalk (¾–4 in), ripening in first autumn. They are egg shaped to oblong, ½–1½ in, set in a cup.

Leaf matte green on upper side, but often covered by honeydew. Underside is pale, waxy bluish green with raised veins.

SIMILAR SPECIES
Quercus frainetto
Leaves of Hungarian oak are larger than oak's, 4–10 in by 2 ⅖–5½ in, with a wedge shaped or slightly ear-like base and about nine pairs of lobes, largest when the leaf is broadest.

Deciduous tree

50–115 ft

This tree is known as English oak and pedunculate oak, from the long stalk or peduncle which carries the acorns. It is native throughout Europe, except the far north, and extends to the east into the Caucasus. In North America it is naturalized in parts of British Columbia in the West and in the Maritime Provinces of Canada (New Brunswick, Prince Edward Island and Nova Scotia) in the East. However, it is widely planted elsewhere as an ornamental or shade tree.

Oak has an excellent timber, which is hard and durable, with an attractive grain. Its appearance is the result of the variation between the less dense spring wood (formed when the tree is growing rapidly in spring and requiring large water vessels to transport water) and the much denser wood formed in summer (when growth is slowed and the tree can make wood that gives strength to the trunk and branches). In oak, the ray cells, which transport material between different growth rings, are larger and more prominent than in most timbers. Hungarian oak is native to southern Italy and the Balkans, distinctive for its large leaves.

138

Quercus robur forms a crown with wide-spreading branches on a stout bole with root buttresses at the base. Young trees have a narrow crown with a single trunk, only broadening when substantive height growth ceases.

BARK
In young trees smooth, gray-green and shiny, becoming increasingly fissured. On old trees it is gray-brown, ridged and furrowed.

Chestnut oak

Quercus prinus

Leaves (5–10 in by 2 ½–4 in) alternate on the shoot. Egg shaped to a narrow ellipse shape, tip drawn out to a broad, blunt point. Margin has regular teeth with rounded, or, less often, acute teeth with ten to fourteen pairs of leaf veins. Upper side is shiny yellow-green, underside is pale with fine hairs. There are pressed-down hairs on the blade and longer hairs on the midrib.

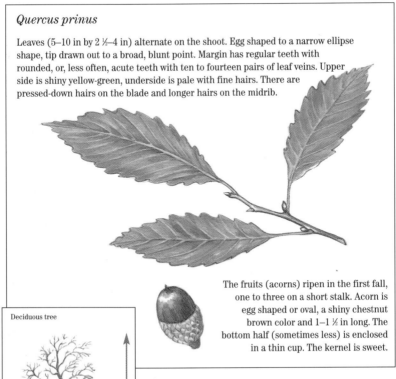

The fruits (acorns) ripen in the first fall, one to three on a short stalk. Acorn is egg shaped or oval, a shiny chestnut brown color and 1–1 ½ in long. The bottom half (sometimes less) is enclosed in a thin cup. The kernel is sweet.

Deciduous tree

50–70 ft, rarely to 100 ft

Chestnut oak grows from southwestern Maine south to Georgia, west just into Mississippi and north to Michigan, with some seen just inside the southernmost tip of Ontario. It makes its best growth on rich lowland soils, but is mainly confined to sandy or gravelly soils, or on dry, rocky, upland sites where it may form pure stands. It provides solid timber and makes a useful shade tree in barren locations. The bark has been used for tanning leather. The name *Quercus montana* is sometimes used for this tree. This is because *Quercus prinus* has been used for both chestnut oak and the related swamp chestnut oak, *Quercus michauxii*. Swamp chestnut oak has a more southerly distribution, from New Jersey to northern Florida and west to eastern Texas. Swamp chestnut oak's leaves are wider than chestnut oak's and their undersides have a soft, velvety feel due to evenly distributed, erect hairs. It is a tree of moist sites, especially along floodplains which are inundated over winter, or beside streams. It grows in mixed forests or in pure stands. The acorns have a similarly sweet kernel, and are tasty either raw or cooked. It is also called cow oak—cows like to eat the acorns.

Quercus prinus makes a medium sized tree with a broad, open crown set on large, ascending limbs.

BARK
Dark gray-brown to black. Thick, with deep furrows and broad, rounded scaly ridges.

Live oak

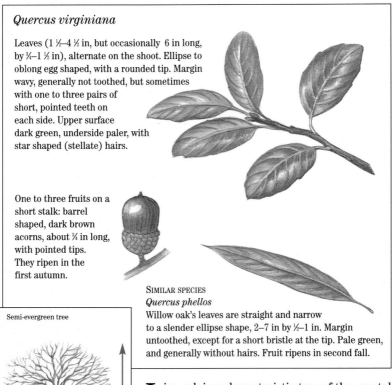

Quercus virginiana

Leaves (1 ½–4 ½ in, but occasionally 6 in long, by ¾–1 ½ in), alternate on the shoot. Ellipse to oblong egg shaped, with a rounded tip. Margin wavy, generally not toothed, but sometimes with one to three pairs of short, pointed teeth on each side. Upper surface dark green, underside paler, with star shaped (stellate) hairs.

One to three fruits on a short stalk: barrel shaped, dark brown acorns, about ¾ in long, with pointed tips. They ripen in the first autumn.

SIMILAR SPECIES
Quercus phellos
Willow oak's leaves are straight and narrow to a slender ellipse shape, 2–7 in by ½–1 in. Margin untoothed, except for a short bristle at the tip. Pale green, and generally without hairs. Fruit ripens in second fall.

Semi-evergreen tree

40–50 ft, rarely to 100 ft

Live oak is a characteristic tree of the coastal plain from North Carolina to Texas. It occurs on seasonally dry sites which are prone to fires, on soils ranging from loams and clays to sands. The trees have crowns forked on low, spreading limbs, and are often much broader than high. The branches are often festooned with Spanish moss. Young trees may have a shrubby phase, during which the tree produces a large, starchy tuber. This is an adaptation to deal with forest fires, giving the tree the energy to make fast new growth after a fire, and thus get ahead of the competition. These tubers have been sliced and fried—like potatoes. The acorns can produce an oil. The wood is hard and heavy, and was used in ships. Live oak is not fully evergreen, but the old leaves fall as the new ones mature. It belongs to the white oak group, as indicated by the fruit maturing in the first fall, after female flowers are pollinated.

Willow oak occurs in a broad arc from southern New York to eastern Texas, extending as far inland as Missouri and Kentucky. It favors moist bottomland sites, along streams and river terraces. It is in the red oak group.

Quercus virginiana forms a wide, spreading tree with a dense, rounded crown set on large spreading branches.

BARK
Dark red-brown, with shallow furrows and flat scaly ridges.

California live oak

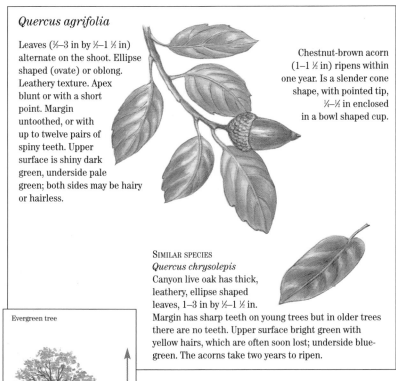

Quercus agrifolia

Leaves (⅜–3 in by ½–1 ½ in)
alternate on the shoot. Ellipse
shaped (ovate) or oblong.
Leathery texture. Apex
blunt or with a short
point. Margin
untoothed, or with
up to twelve pairs of
spiny teeth. Upper
surface is shiny dark
green, underside pale
green; both sides may be hairy
or hairless.

Chestnut-brown acorn
(1–1 ½ in) ripens within
one year. Is a slender cone
shape, with pointed tip,
¼–½ in enclosed
in a bowl shaped cup.

SIMILAR SPECIES
Quercus chrysolepis
Canyon live oak has thick,
leathery, ellipse shaped
leaves, 1–3 in by ½–1 ½ in.
Margin has sharp teeth on young trees but in older trees
there are no teeth. Upper surface bright green with
yellow hairs, which are often soon lost; underside blue-
green. The acorns take two years to ripen.

Evergreen tree

50–75 ft

California live oak is found along the coastal
ranges from Sonoma County and extends south
into northern Baja California. It is slow growing,
intolerant of shade and found on hillside slopes or
in valley bottoms, but generally on dry sites. It
forms open parkland groves, either as pure stands or with other oaks. The name
'live oak' refers to the evergreen foliage. Although the tree is never leafless, the
leaves persist only until the new set is formed. Despite the bitter flesh of the
acorn, it was a favored food of Native Americans. They ground the flesh into a
meal and then soaked it to remove the bitter element. This was then boiled to
make bread. Canyon live oak is found in Arizona, New Mexico, Nevada, California,
southwestern Oregon and northern Mexico. It occurs on mountain ridges, moist
slopes and along canyons. The amount of hair on the leaves is extremely variable.
They are golden and have several arms; you will need a hand lens to see this. This
hairiness makes canyon live oak one of the most attractive of the Californian
oaks: the Latin name translates as 'golden scales'. The wood is hard and heavy
and was used for wheel axles and for mauls for splitting redwoods.

Quercus agrifolia forms an evergreen tree with an irregular spreading crown set on a framework of stout branches.

BARK
Light gray to nearly black, thick and becoming deeply furrowed into scaly ridges.

Northern red oak

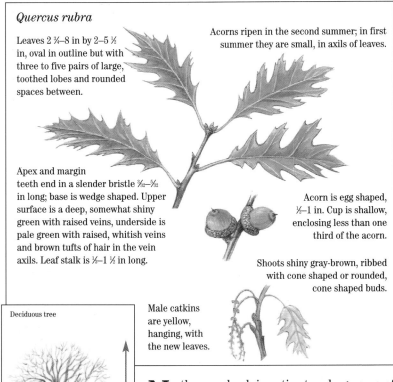

Quercus rubra

Leaves 2 ¾–8 in by 2–5 ½ in, oval in outline but with three to five pairs of large, toothed lobes and rounded spaces between.

Acorns ripen in the second summer; in first summer they are small, in axils of leaves.

Apex and margin teeth end in a slender bristle ³⁄₃₂–⁵⁄₃₂ in long; base is wedge shaped. Upper surface is a deep, somewhat shiny green with raised veins, underside is pale green with raised, whitish veins and brown tufts of hair in the vein axils. Leaf stalk is ⅙–1 ½ in long.

Acorn is egg shaped, ½–1 in. Cup is shallow, enclosing less than one third of the acorn.

Shoots shiny gray-brown, ribbed with cone shaped or rounded, cone shaped buds.

Deciduous tree

66–82 ft

Male catkins are yellow, hanging, with the new leaves.

Northern red oak is native to a large area of eastern North America from the southern side of the St. Lawrence River west to Minnesota and south to Oklahoma and Georgia. It is the most widely distributed of the red oaks, and forms a large tree. The timber is used for flooring, furniture, planking and pulpwood. It is a fast-growing oak and transplants easily. Northern red oak thrives on acidic sands or rocky soils where it forms pure stands, and also on clays, but it does not thrive on shallow soils over chalk. The main branches radiate out from the trunk. The foliage often turns an impressive red in autumn, covering the entire crown at the same time. This gives rise to both the common and scientific names, but some trees make nothing better than a poor brown. If buying one from a nursery, make your choice when the tree is in autumn color in order to select the best. The new foliage in spring is yellow for several days.

Red oak is a member of an entirely American section of the genus, characterized by the bristle-like tips to the teeth or side lobes of the leaves. (The bristles are made by the veins extending beyond the end of the leaf.)

Quercus rubra forms a tall, wide
tree with big, spreading branches.
The crown is more open than
on other oaks and allows
dappled sunlight to penetrate
to the forest floor.

BARK
Silvery gray or dark gray
and smooth in young trees,
developing scaly ridges
in old trees and showing
the red inner bark in
the fissures.

Scarlet oak

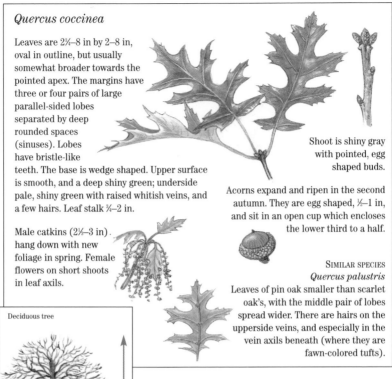

Quercus coccinea

Leaves are 2¾–8 in by 2–8 in, oval in outline, but usually somewhat broader towards the pointed apex. The margins have three or four pairs of large parallel-sided lobes separated by deep rounded spaces (sinuses). Lobes have bristle-like teeth. The base is wedge shaped. Upper surface is smooth, and a deep shiny green; underside pale, shiny green with raised whitish veins, and a few hairs. Leaf stalk ¾–2 in.

Male catkins (2⅓–3 in) hang down with new foliage in spring. Female flowers on short shoots in leaf axils.

Deciduous tree

66–98 ft

Shoot is shiny gray with pointed, egg shaped buds.

Acorns expand and ripen in the second autumn. They are egg shaped, ½–1 in, and sit in an open cup which encloses the lower third to a half.

SIMILAR SPECIES
Quercus palustris
Leaves of pin oak smaller than scarlet oak's, with the middle pair of lobes spread wider. There are hairs on the upperside veins, and especially in the vein axils beneath (where they are fawn-colored tufts).

Scarlet oak is native to eastern North America from Maine south to Georgia and west to Mississippi and Indiana, where it is found in forests on poor soils from thin sands to upland ridges. Like northern red oak (page 146) its leaf veins extend beyond the end of the leaf blade as slender filaments. However, it is most easily separated from red oak by the deep and regular spaces (sinuses) between the leaf lobes and the almost hairless, shinier leaves. The branch structure does not have the heavy radiating main branches of red oak, but tends to be more upright, with more twigs in the crown. Both the common name and scientific name refer to the scarlet autumn color.

Pin oak, *Quercus palustris*, is native to eastern North America from Vermont across to southern Ontario and Iowa south to Oklahoma and South Carolina, where it occurs in swamps and seasonally flooded sites (the scientific name means marshy). The acorn is nearly round and sits on a saucer-shaped cup enclosing the lower third to a quarter. The crown's lower branches hang down.

148

Brilliant in autumn color, *Quercus coccinea* forms a large tree with a tall, domed crown. The branch structure lacks the heavy, radiating main branches of northern red oak (page 146) and the tree tends to be more upright, with a twiggy crown.

BARK
Silver-gray to dark gray, smooth but with warts. As the tree matures it becomes fissured into fine, scaly ridges revealing the red inner bark.

Black oak

Quercus velutina

Leaves (4–10 in by 3–6 in) alternate on the shoot, oval to egg shaped (obovate). Apex ends in a thin spine-like bristle. Margin has three or four pairs of lobes ending in a few bristle-tipped teeth. Shiny green above, yellow-green underneath, and often with brown hairs.

Acorn (½–⅞₆ in) ripens in the second autumn. It is egg shaped to nearly round, the lower half enclosed in a cup which has red-brown, hairy scales loosely pressed down on it.

SIMILAR SPECIES
Quercus marilandica
Black-jack oak has wedge shaped leaves (2 ½–5 in by 2–4 in), broadest near the rather truncated tip, which has three shallow, bristle-tipped lobes.

Deciduous tree

Up to 80 ft

Black oak's range is from Maine south to Florida, across to central Texas and from there north into Minnesota, just extending into southern Ontario. It is characteristic of dry, sandy or rocky ridges, or poorly drained uplands.

The name black oak is from the color of the bark of mature trees. However, it is also known as quercitron oak or yellow oak, names referring to the inner bark. This is yellow or orange. It is very bitter due to the high tannin content and was formerly used for tanning leather. The bark can also be dried and pounded to give a yellow dye, quercitron (literally 'oak lemon').

Black-jack oak was first named in Maryland (hence 'marilandica'). It is a small tree, often no more than 30 feet high. In Texas and Oklahoma it occurs at the transition zone between woodland and prairie.

These two species belong to the red oak group of oaks, which occurs only in the Americas, characterized by the acorns, which usually take two years to ripen, and by the dense, hairy layer on the inside of the acorn. In all, there are 35 species of red oak in North America.

Quercus velutina develops an irregularly domed crown in old trees, with large spreading branches. Younger trees are usually cone shaped.

BARK
Rough, thick and blackish when mature and furrowing into plates. Illustrated here is *Quercus marilandica*.

Tanoak

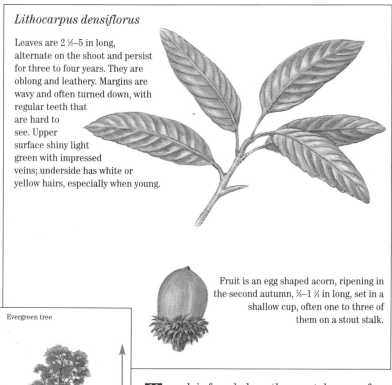

Lithocarpus densiflorus

Leaves are 2 ½–5 in long, alternate on the shoot and persist for three to four years. They are oblong and leathery. Margins are wavy and often turned down, with regular teeth that are hard to see. Upper surface shiny light green with impressed veins; underside has white or yellow hairs, especially when young.

Fruit is an egg shaped acorn, ripening in the second autumn, ¾–1 ¼ in long, set in a shallow cup, often one to three of them on a stout stalk.

Evergreen tree

50–80 ft occasionally up to 135 ft

Tanoak is found along the coastal ranges from mid Oregon to southern California, where it grows in moist, well-drained sites or on mountain slopes. It is found either with conifers and other hardwoods or, less often, in pure stands. This is a long-lived tree with a deep root system. In California's Sierra Nevada there is a variety, var. *echinoides,* which has smaller, flat leaves, no more than 2 ½ in long. This makes a shrub of only 10 ft or so.

Tanoak used to be important as the only western source of tannin. The nuts seem very similar to the acorns of oaks (*Quercus*), but the structure of the flowering catkin shows that the species is more closely related to *Castanea* and *Chrysolepis*, with rudimentary female flowers at the base of the erect male catkin. The name *Lithocarpus* translates as 'stone fruit' and refers to the thick shell around the nut. The genus contains over one hundred species in eastern Asia, but only the one in America. The acorns have a bitter flavor. Native Americans used to make a flour by removing the shells and washing the kernels in hot water to remove the bitterness.

Lithocarpus densiflorus makes a bold, evergreen tree on a central trunk, ranging from narrow conical to broad and rounded.

BARK
Thick, gray or brown, deeply fissured into scaly ridges but smooth in young trees.

Golden chinkapin

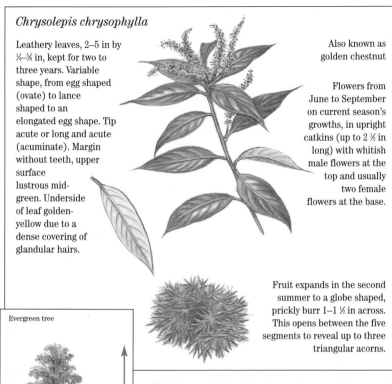

Chrysolepis chrysophylla

Leathery leaves, 2–5 in by ¼–⅝ in, kept for two to three years. Variable shape, from egg shaped (ovate) to lance shaped to an elongated egg shape. Tip acute or long and acute (acuminate). Margin without teeth, upper surface lustrous mid-green. Underside of leaf golden-yellow due to a dense covering of glandular hairs.

Also known as golden chestnut

Flowers from June to September on current season's growths, in upright catkins (up to 2 ½ in long) with whitish male flowers at the top and usually two female flowers at the base.

Fruit expands in the second summer to a globe shaped, prickly burr 1–1 ½ in across. This opens between the five segments to reveal up to three triangular acorns.

Evergreen tree

Up to 80 ft

Golden chinkapin is native to the coastal ranges of northern California, Oregon and southwestern Washington, where it grows in mixed evergreen forest, with the coastal redwood, or in conifer forest. On the best sites, it can make 135 ft, but is usually only 60–80 ft. At the southern end of its range, there is a variety, var. *minor*, which has an obtuse or rounded tip to the leaves and a thin, smooth bark. This form grows on drier, rocky or gravelly sites on open slopes with pines; it also grows in chaparral, where it makes no more than a shrubby tree, up to about 30 ft in height; this extends the range into the Sierra Nevada of central California.

The female flowers at the base of the catkin are a distinguishing feature that golden chinkapin shares with *Castanea*, or chestnut, and it was originally considered to be in this genus.

The genus name is from the Greek for golden (*chrysos*) and scales (*lepis*), and refers to the covering of golden scales on most parts of the tree.

Chrysolepis chrysophylla forms a tree with a dense, rounded crown set on stout, spreading branches when growing on fertile and moist sites, but on drier sites is often more of a shrub.

BARK
Thick, deeply furrowed, and dark red-brown with bright red inner bark. Gray and smooth in young trees.

American chestnut

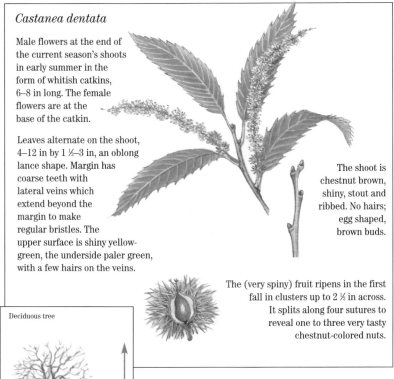

Castanea dentata

Male flowers at the end of the current season's shoots in early summer in the form of whitish catkins, 6–8 in long. The female flowers are at the base of the catkin.

Leaves alternate on the shoot, 4–12 in by 1 ½–3 in, an oblong lance shape. Margin has coarse teeth with lateral veins which extend beyond the margin to make regular bristles. The upper surface is shiny yellow-green, the underside paler green, with a few hairs on the veins.

The shoot is chestnut brown, shiny, stout and ribbed. No hairs; egg shaped, brown buds.

The (very spiny) fruit ripens in the first fall in clusters up to 2 ½ in across. It splits along four sutures to reveal one to three very tasty chestnut-colored nuts.

Deciduous tree

Up to 30 ft

American chestnut is native to the eastern side of the continent from Maine southwest to Louisiana, and north to Wisconsin and southern Ontario. It was widely planted within this zone because of its nuts, and before the early 1900s was a dominant tree in eastern hardwood forests, where it grew on moist upland soils, reaching 100 ft. However, in 1904 chestnut blight was introduced to New York State and over the next three decades spread across the country. The blight, caused by the fungus *Cryphonectria parasitica* (syn. *Endothia parasitica*), destroys the tree, leaving only vigorous sprout shoots. These generally survive for a number of years before being struck down by the blight, then sprouting again in a vegetative cycle. Only occasionally do these sprouts grow large enough to fruit.

Chestnuts from China and Japan are resistant to the disease, and are still planted for their nuts. They are cross-bred with American chestnut, the aim being to breed in resistance to the blight.

Castanea dentata used to make an upright, domed tree, but chestnut blight has restricted it to small, shrub-like growths.

BARK
Where old trees have survived chestnut blight, bark becomes fissured into flat ridges as illustrated. Most commonly seen is bark that is smooth on young stems and sprouts, dark gray-brown.

American beech

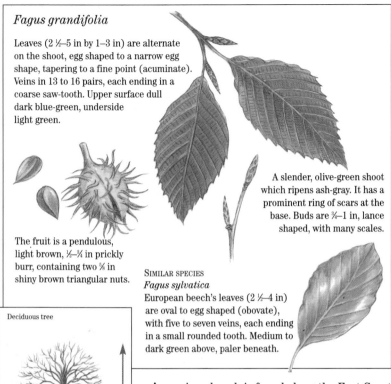

Fagus grandifolia

Leaves (2 ½–5 in by 1–3 in) are alternate on the shoot, egg shaped to a narrow egg shape, tapering to a fine point (acuminate). Veins in 13 to 16 pairs, each ending in a coarse saw-tooth. Upper surface dull dark blue-green, underside light green.

A slender, olive-green shoot which ripens ash-gray. It has a prominent ring of scars at the base. Buds are ¾–1 in, lance shaped, with many scales.

The fruit is a pendulous, light brown, ½–¾ in prickly burr, containing two ⅝ in shiny brown triangular nuts.

SIMILAR SPECIES
Fagus sylvatica
European beech's leaves (2 ½–4 in) are oval to egg shaped (obovate), with five to seven veins, each ending in a small rounded tooth. Medium to dark green above, paler beneath.

Deciduous tree

70 ft, occasionally to 100 ft

American beech is found along the East Coast from New England south to northern Florida, and west to eastern Texas and Wisconsin. In Canada it occurs in Nova Scotia, New Brunswick and Prince Edward Island, and across southern Quebec to southern Ontario. It thrives on rich soils in either hardwood or mixed conifer and broadleaved forests. It is not deep-rooting, and does not do well on dry sites. It will sprout or sucker from the roots.

The nuts are edible and much favored by squirrels, raccoon and other wildlife. The timber is strong and hard, but not durable if used outside. However, it has a light color and is excellent for flooring or for furniture.

European beech is often planted in parks or used for hedging—it tolerates clipping. It makes a similar, bold tree, easily identified by its leaves, which have far fewer veins than American beech and small, rounded teeth. The new leaves are a bright, fresh green but soon darken until they turn yellow-brown in the fall. The tree has produced a large number of horticultural variants, the most familiar being those with purple or copper foliage.

Fagus grandifolia makes a large tree with a crown composed of long, spreading branches.

BARK
Blue-gray or silvery gray, often mottled. It is smooth, remaining so through the tree's life, only rarely becoming fissured and corky.

American elm

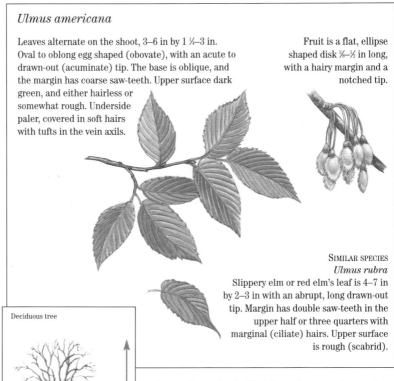

Ulmus americana

Leaves alternate on the shoot, 3–6 in by 1 ¼–3 in. Oval to oblong egg shaped (obovate), with an acute to drawn-out (acuminate) tip. The base is oblique, and the margin has coarse saw-teeth. Upper surface dark green, and either hairless or somewhat rough. Underside paler, covered in soft hairs with tufts in the vein axils.

Fruit is a flat, ellipse shaped disk ⅜–½ in long, with a hairy margin and a notched tip.

SIMILAR SPECIES
Ulmus rubra
Slippery elm or red elm's leaf is 4–7 in by 2–3 in with an abrupt, long drawn-out tip. Margin has double saw-teeth in the upper half or three quarters with marginal (ciliate) hairs. Upper surface is rough (scabrid).

Deciduous tree

60–100 ft.

American elm is distributed across the eastern half of the continent and is native to the territory to the south and east of a line drawn between central Texas north to central-eastern Saskatchewan and from there eastwards to Prince Edward Island, but excluding southern Florida. In the wild it grows on moist soils, such as along rivers and in swamp forests, also in deciduous woodland with other hardwood trees. Widely planted as a shade tree in towns, it grows fast and makes a pleasing vase shape. It is becoming naturalized in parts of the West, especially in Idaho and Arizona, but has suffered badly from Dutch elm disease which has destroyed most large trees within its natural distribution. The disease is caused by a fungus which is spread by bark beetles. The wood is hard and used for furniture and paneling. Slippery elm has a similar range, from central Texas north to North Dakota and then east to Maine via southern Ontario and Quebec. It is only in the far northwest of Florida, and is missing from much of Georgia. The upper leaf surfaces are much rougher than American elm's. The name is derived from the slipper, or mucilaginous inner bark, of both twigs and trunks.

Ulnus americana forms a tall tree with a single stem which forks into many spreading stems, drooping at the tips, like a vase full of neatly arranged flowers.

BARK
Light brown to gray and deeply fissured into plates on old trees.

161

Wych elm or Scotch elm

Ulmus glabra

Leaves oval to elongated oval, 3–7 in by 1 ½–4 in. Apex slender and pointed, often with a broad shoulder, or with three (or more) large, triangular lobes. Margin has coarse double teeth. Base is very oblique—markedly different on the two sides. Upper surface very rough with fourteen to twenty pairs of impressed veins, underside hairy with raised veins. Leaf stalk less than ¼ in.

Purplish-red flowers appear before the leaves in late winter.

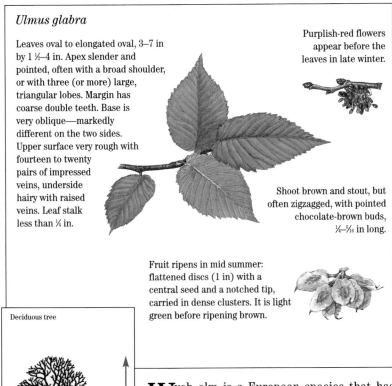

Shoot brown and stout, but often zigzagged, with pointed chocolate-brown buds, ¼–⁵⁄₁₆ in long.

Fruit ripens in mid summer: flattened discs (1 in) with a central seed and a notched tip, carried in dense clusters. It is light green before ripening brown.

Deciduous tree

66–98 ft

Wych elm is a European species that has been planted in most states. It is naturalized in British Columbia and California, and in Connecticut, New York, Rhode Island, Maine, Massachusetts and Vermont, and perhaps elsewhere. It is similar to red elm (page 160), differing in the smooth trunk and the fruits not being hairy.

This is the only elm which is clearly native to Britain and the only one which reproduces entirely from seed, unlike English elm and smooth-leaved elm, which rely upon root suckers. Wych elm has a reasonable timber, once used for coffins and furniture, but the devastation caused by Dutch elm disease has made the timber less readily available. Another historical use for the timber was to make water pipes—the wood lasts indefinitely if kept wet and wych elm pipes survive from Roman times. The scientific name, *glabra*, translates as smooth and is often used in the sense of hairless. The leaves of wych elm, however, are rough to the touch and hairy on the underside. The smoothness in this case refers to the bark, which remains so, at least for several years.

The rounded, domed crown is enhanced in late winter by the purplish male flowers, and in autumn by an attractive yellow.

BARK
Smooth and silvery gray for a number of years, then becoming gray-brown and fissured with interconnecting ridges.

Japanese zelkova

Zelkova serrata

Leaves alternate on the shoot, egg shaped to lance shaped, 1–4¾ in by ½–1½ in. They taper to an acute tip. Base rounded, with six to thirteen large, coarse triangular teeth. Dark green above, paler beneath and hairy on both sides: leaf stalk round, ⅟₃₂ in.

Shoots are slender and have silky hairs when young. They mature to gray-brown, with small, egg shaped buds (⅟₃₂ in).

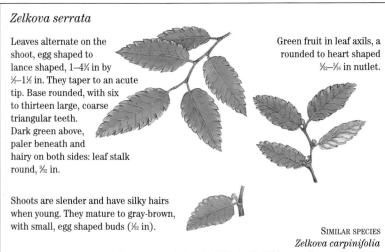

Green fruit in leaf axils, a rounded to heart shaped ⁵⁄₃₂–³⁄₁₆ in nutlet.

SIMILAR SPECIES
Zelkova carpinifolia

Caucasian elm's leaves are oblong, 1–3½ in by ½–1½ in, usually rounded at the tip and at the base, which is uneven—see illustration. The margins have rounded teeth with a small abrupt point. Side veins fork, with one side running to the point and the other to the sinus or space between the teeth.

Fruit of Caucasian elm is egg shaped, ribbed, ³⁄₁₆–¼ in.

Deciduous tree

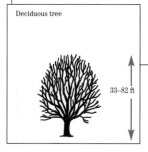

33–82 ft

Japanese zelkova is native to the southern part of Japan, to Taiwan and to mainland Asia in Korea and northeast China. It can make a large tree, but is most often seen in recent plantings where it is rather flat topped and broader than high. It is grown in North America only as an ornamental, or shade tree, being planted across the continent. *Keaki* is the Japanese name.

Caucasian elm is native from eastern Turkey to Armenia and Georgia, and to northern Iran on the southern side of the Caspian Sea. It makes an erect growing tree with many ascending stems arranged like the pipes of an organ. It frequently has a stout trunk or bole with many ascending stems arranged like the pipes of an organ.

The two species can easily be separated by the rounded teeth of *carpinifolia*, as opposed to the triangular teeth of *serrata*. Zelkova is closely related to the elms (*Ulmus*) and hackberries (*Celtis*). From elms, it differs in the fruit being a drupe, like in hackberry. However, from hackberry it differs most obviously in the leaf veins—these are pinnate, i.e. branch off the midrib, not basal as in *Celtis*.

Zelkova serrata makes a spreading, small tree, green and leafy during summer and a mixture of yellow, orange and pink in autumn.

BARK
Smooth and gray with prominent pink, orange or brown breathing pores (lenticels).

Hackberry

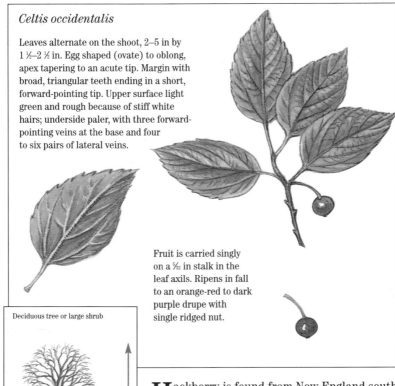

Celtis occidentalis

Leaves alternate on the shoot, 2–5 in by 1 ½–2 ½ in. Egg shaped (ovate) to oblong, apex tapering to an acute tip. Margin with broad, triangular teeth ending in a short, forward-pointing tip. Upper surface light green and rough because of stiff white hairs; underside paler, with three forward-pointing veins at the base and four to six pairs of lateral veins.

Fruit is carried singly on a ⁵⁄₃₂ in stalk in the leaf axils. Ripens in fall to an orange-red to dark purple drupe with single ridged nut.

Deciduous tree or large shrub

30–90 ft

Hackberry is found from New England south to Georgia and west to Oklahoma and the Dakotas, with scattered populations extending the range into Quebec and Manitoba. It is mainly found in river valleys, where the tallest trees occur. But it also grows on uplands and bluffs, where it is tolerant to drought, making a smaller, even shrub-like tree.

Hackberry is often planted as a shade tree, particularly in the West, where its drought tolerance is valued. The fruit, a drupe, is a useful food for wildlife. Drupes have a hard, stony layer around the seed with an outer fleshy layer. The fleshy layer in hackberry is dry but sweet, and the name comes from the Scots 'hagberry', meaning marsh cherry.

Celtis is a large genus, with sixty to a hundred species. They all have the prominent three veins from the base of the leaf. Five other species are native to the U.S.A. Of these, *Celtis laevigata* and *C. tenuifolia* occur largely to the southeast of the hackberry's range, while *C. reticulata* occurs in the western states.

Celtis occidentalis makes a domed tree with a rounded, spreading, or slightly pendent crown on better sites. On dry sites, it is often shrub-like with several stems.

BARK
Gray and smooth, but becoming roughened with warty growths or long, narrow ridges; scaly in old trees.

Red and white mulberry

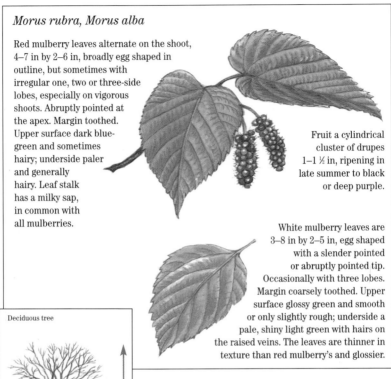

Morus rubra, Morus alba

Red mulberry leaves alternate on the shoot, 4–7 in by 2–6 in, broadly egg shaped in outline, but sometimes with irregular one, two or three-side lobes, especially on vigorous shoots. Abruptly pointed at the apex. Margin toothed. Upper surface dark blue-green and sometimes hairy; underside paler and generally hairy. Leaf stalk has a milky sap, in common with all mulberries.

Fruit a cylindrical cluster of drupes 1–1 ½ in, ripening in late summer to black or deep purple.

White mulberry leaves are 3–8 in by 2–5 in, egg shaped with a slender pointed or abruptly pointed tip. Occasionally with three lobes. Margin coarsely toothed. Upper surface glossy green and smooth or only slightly rough; underside a pale, shiny light green with hairs on the raised veins. The leaves are thinner in texture than red mulberry's and glossier.

Deciduous tree

30–65 ft

Red mulberry is native to the eastern half of the country, from southeastern Minnesota across to southern Ontario and Massachusetts and south to Florida and central Texas. It grows on moist soils in hardwood forests up to 2,000 ft. The berries are technically a syncarp—a cluster of separate fruits. When ripe, they are tasty—much appreciated by wildlife—and will stain the fingers purple. The inner bark was used by Native Americans as a fiber and woven into cloaks. White mulberry is a native of China, where it has been grown for centuries as the favored food of the silkworm grub. The first white mulberries were imported to America in an attempt to start a silk industry—but it failed. Despite this, the tree itself has not looked back; it is now naturalized over most of the eastern half of the continent and is spreading in the Southwest. Wild animals appreciate the fruits, and humans the shade. It does not make as large a tree as red mulberry and is less demanding about site conditions. Black mulberry, *Morus nigra*, is another Chinese species grown as a shade and as a fruit tree. The leaves are similar to red mulberry's, but rougher on the upper surface; and heart shaped at the base.

Morus rubra or *Morus alba* makes a broad, rounded, leafy crown on a short trunk.

BARK
Mulberry bark: orange-brown or light brown, developing fissures and scaly or stringy ridges.

Black or rum cherry

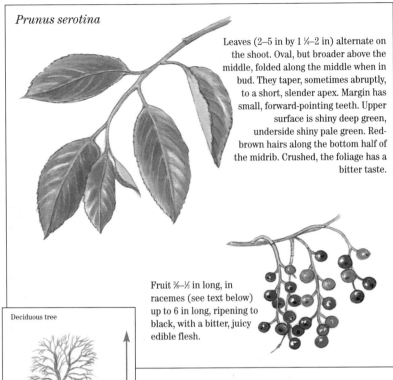

Prunus serotina

Leaves (2–5 in by 1 ¼–2 in) alternate on the shoot. Oval, but broader above the middle, folded along the middle when in bud. They taper, sometimes abruptly, to a short, slender apex. Margin has small, forward-pointing teeth. Upper surface is shiny deep green, underside shiny pale green. Red-brown hairs along the bottom half of the midrib. Crushed, the foliage has a bitter taste.

Fruit ⅜–½ in long, in racemes (see text below) up to 6 in long, ripening to black, with a bitter, juicy edible flesh.

Deciduous tree

Up to 80 ft

Black or rum cherry is found across the eastern half of the continent from Nova Scotia to Florida and west to the Dakotas and Texas. It thrives on a wide range of sites, only avoiding the wettest or driest. Its most distinctive feature is the line of red-brown hairs which lie along the bottom half of the midrib on the underside. It is also often suggested that black cherry extends through Mexico south to Ecuador, but these trees are better considered as a related species, *Prunus salicifolia*, which differs in having leathery, not hairy, leaves that are lance shaped and broadest below the middle. Black cherry belongs to the subgenus *Padus*, which has its flowers and fruits in a leafy raceme (an arrangement of flowers which are carried on stalks off a common central axis). The leaves are folded along the middle when in bud. There is usually a pair of glands at the base of the leaf blade or at the top of the leaf stalk. These are 'extra-floral nectaries', which secrete sugars that attract ants. The ants eat any other bugs, which otherwise would eat the leaves. The wood is decorative and hard, used for paneling and for furniture. A cough medicine can be made from the bark.

Prunus serotina makes an upright tree with an oblong or irregular crown and spreading or ascending branches.

BARK
Rough, dark purplish-gray to black. Peels in small strips. Older specimens have thick, ridged bark.

171

Birdcherry

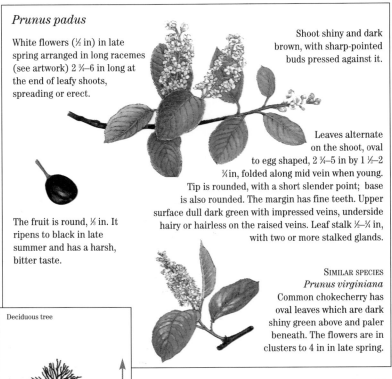

Prunus padus

White flowers (½ in) in late spring arranged in long racemes (see artwork) 2 ¾–6 in long at the end of leafy shoots, spreading or erect.

Shoot shiny and dark brown, with sharp-pointed buds pressed against it.

Leaves alternate on the shoot, oval to egg shaped, 2 ¾–5 in by 1 ½–2 ¾ in, folded along mid vein when young. Tip is rounded, with a short slender point; base is also rounded. The margin has fine teeth. Upper surface dull dark green with impressed veins, underside hairy or hairless on the raised veins. Leaf stalk ½–¾ in, with two or more stalked glands.

The fruit is round, ⅓ in. It ripens to black in late summer and has a harsh, bitter taste.

SIMILAR SPECIES
Prunus virginiana
Common chokecherry has oval leaves which are dark shiny green above and paler beneath. The flowers are in clusters to 4 in in late spring.

Deciduous tree

33–66 ft

This cherry is grown as an ornamental and is naturalized in some places in North America. Its native range is Europe except for the Balkans, and it extends almost to the far north of Norway and Sweden. It is also native across Siberia into northeastern China and into the northern Japanese island of Hokkaido. Unsuited to hot or dry sites, it prefers cool, moist places.

Birdcherry contains cyanide in the leaves, fruits and wood—to some extent a feature of all *Prunus* species. Only in a few species, for example bitter almonds, is the quantity enough to be dangerous.

Common chokecherry is extremely widely spread, from Labrador west across Canada to British Columbia and south to a wavy line running from North Carolina to California but avoiding the Southeast coastal plain and Texas. It grows in moist soils beside streams and in clearings in mountain forests. It is usually a shrub—up to 20 feet or so. The fruit has a bitter flesh but when fully ripe can be used for preserves. The stone and also the foliage is rich in cyanide, making wilted foliage potentially dangerous to cattle and other stock.

Prunus padus is planted as an ornamental tree for its showy white flowers. They can almost obliterate the leaves. It is frequently wider than tall when planted as an ornamental.

BARK
Dark gray-brown and smooth, becoming fissured. If cut, it smells acrid.

Sweetcherry

Prunus avium

Fruit (¾ in) ripens in mid summer. It is round, with a juicy covering over the hard, bony seed, ripening to blackish red or yellow-red.

Leaves alternate on the shoot, oblong to oval, 2 ¾–4 ¾ in by 1 ½–2 in, folded along the mid vein when young. Tip has a slender point. The base is rounded or wedge shaped, and the margin has sharp saw-teeth. Upper surface dark green; underside paler, with hairs on the raised veins. Leaf stalk ¾–1 ⅛ in, with two to five stalked glands.

Shoot is shiny purple-brown, with bluntly pointed egg shaped buds, ³⁄₁₆ in long.

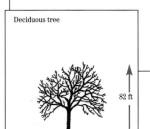

White flowers in mid spring in small clusters with the new foliage, hanging down, 1–1 ⅛ in.

Deciduous tree

82 ft

Sweetcherry or mazzard is widely planted across the continent for its fruit and has become naturalized in southeastern Canada and in the U.S.A. in both the East and the Northwest. Its native distribution is throughout Europe, south into North Africa and east to Turkey and Iran. The fruit can be either sweet or bitter, but is not acid. This is the parent tree for the sweetcherry varieties used in orchards worldwide. The scientific name translates as birdcherry—confusing, since the common name of *Prunus padus*, page 172, is birdcherry.

The tree grows on a range of soils, but on dry, sandy ones it tends to be short lived. The largest trees develop on moisture-retentive clays or loams and can be nearly as big as oak in mixed woodland. The hard, light red timber is excellent, and used for furniture, flooring and sculpture; it sells for more than oak. The seed has a hard case and requires two treatments to germinate. First, a moist, warm period to break down the case; then a cool one to remove the chemicals which inhibit germination. As the seeds ripen in the summer, they can get the first, but often need a second summer to complete the second.

Prunus avium makes a very attractive sight in spring when in full flower and can brighten mixed woodland, orchards or gardens. Branches of young trees are in spaced whorls; on older trees, the crown is rounded, dense and twiggy.

BARK
Shiny, purplish red and peeling slightly in young trees. There are prominent breathing pores (lenticels). Older trees develop gray or black fissures.

Japanese cherry

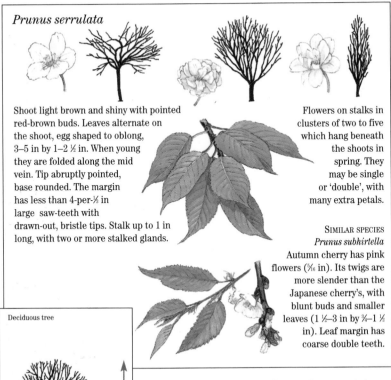

Prunus serrulata

Shoot light brown and shiny with pointed red-brown buds. Leaves alternate on the shoot, egg shaped to oblong, 3–5 in by 1–2 ½ in. When young they are folded along the mid vein. Tip abruptly pointed, base rounded. The margin has less than 4-per-⅓ in large saw-teeth with drawn-out, bristle tips. Stalk up to 1 in long, with two or more stalked glands.

Flowers on stalks in clusters of two to five which hang beneath the shoots in spring. They may be single or 'double', with many extra petals.

SIMILAR SPECIES
Prunus subhirtella
Autumn cherry has pink flowers (⁵⁄₁₆ in). Its twigs are more slender than the Japanese cherry's, with blunt buds and smaller leaves (1 ½–3 in by ¾–1 ½ in). Leaf margin has coarse double teeth.

Deciduous tree

33 ft

Japanese cherry is native to the mountains of Japan, also to central and northern China and Korea. In these isolated areas the trees vary and are usually assigned to different varieties. The wild tree tends to have excellent autumn color, but the garden forms are less reliable, selected firstly for their gaudy flowers.

A selection of the garden forms, or *sato zakura* (Japanese for garden cherries), would include: 'Amanogawa', with erect branches making a narrow upright tree up to 26 ft with pale pink flowers; 'Kanzan', with purplish-pink flowers on a semi-erect vase-shaped crown; 'Shirofugen', with arching, hanging branches and deep rose-pink double flowers which fade to dull whitish pink; 'Shirotae', with a spreading crown and intense white hanging flowers; 'Tai Haku' with large, white single flowers, largest in the group; and 'Ukon', with curious greenish-yellow flowers.

Prunus subhirtella is mainly grown as the autumn cherry, 'Autumnalis', giving a succession of flowers in mild periods from late autumn. 'Rosea' normally flowers in spring.

Prunus serrulata occurs in a large range of flower and habit forms. The crown varies from the narrow upright of 'Amanogawa' to the spreading 'Ukon' and 'Tai Haku'. In 'Kanzan' the crown is a semi-erect vase shape, but droops on old trees.

BARK
Brown, with prominent horizontal lenticels or breathing pores, smooth in young trees but rougher in old trees.

Pear

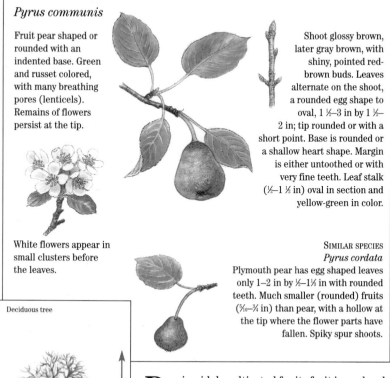

Pyrus communis

Fruit pear shaped or rounded with an indented base. Green and russet colored, with many breathing pores (lenticels). Remains of flowers persist at the tip.

White flowers appear in small clusters before the leaves.

Deciduous tree

39–82 ft

Shoot glossy brown, later gray brown, with shiny, pointed red-brown buds. Leaves alternate on the shoot, a rounded egg shape to oval, 1 ½–3 in by 1 ½–2 in; tip rounded or with a short point. Base is rounded or a shallow heart shape. Margin is either untoothed or with very fine teeth. Leaf stalk (½–1 ½ in) oval in section and yellow-green in color.

SIMILAR SPECIES
Pyrus cordata
Plymouth pear has egg shaped leaves only 1–2 in by ½–1⅛ in with rounded teeth. Much smaller (rounded) fruits (⁵⁄₁₆–¾ in) than pear, with a hollow at the tip where the flower parts have fallen. Spiky spur shoots.

Pear is widely cultivated for its fruit in orchards throughout North America and occasionally seedlings are found in woods. It was introduced in colonial times from Europe. However, it is not clear where it originated, and it is possible that the orchard pear, as described here, is actually a complex hybrid involving several pear species from southern and Eastern Europe and western Asia.

The orchard varieties comprise several hundred different forms, all varying in their fruit size, texture, ripening and taste. However, they share the leathery, glossy leaves. Pears have thick-walled cells (grit cells) in the fruits, which are not found in orchard apples. The fruit tends to ripen rather quickly and is very juicy—best eaten over the kitchen sink. The fruits can be fermented to make perry and this is distilled to make calvados.

Plymouth pear is a small tree, mainly found from western France south into Spain and Portugal, and is occasionally grown in North America. There are a few trees in old hedgerows near Plymouth in Devon and Truro in Cornwall, and it may be native there.

Pyrus communis is most attractive in early spring when flowering before the leaves expand. It makes an upright, small to medium tree, spiky when young, but dense and leafy with a rounded crown when old.

BARK
Brown or black, quickly becoming cracked into small square plates or scales.

179

Crabapple

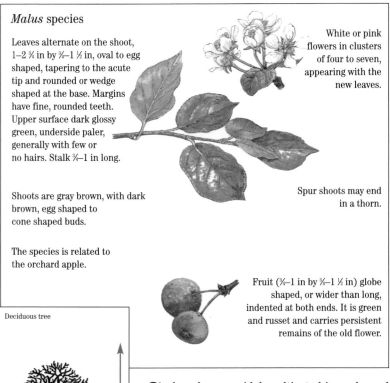

Malus species

Leaves alternate on the shoot, 1–2 ¾ in by ¾–1 ½ in, oval to egg shaped, tapering to the acute tip and rounded or wedge shaped at the base. Margins have fine, rounded teeth. Upper surface dark glossy green, underside paler, generally with few or no hairs. Stalk ¾–1 in long.

White or pink flowers in clusters of four to seven, appearing with the new leaves.

Shoots are gray brown, with dark brown, egg shaped to cone shaped buds.

Spur shoots may end in a thorn.

The species is related to the orchard apple.

Fruit (¾–1 in by ¾–1 ½ in) globe shaped, or wider than long, indented at both ends. It is green and russet and carries persistent remains of the old flower.

Deciduous tree

33–49 ft

Crabapples are widely cultivated in parks and gardens. There are several dozen different cultivars. They are grown for their flowers—masses and masses shroud the small trees in spring. Some are also grown for their autumn color.

Several different species are found in gardens or in natural forest, plus many hybrids. The species illustrated is the European crabapple which may be naturalized in southern Canada and in eastern and western U.S.A.. The leaves are rolled up in the buds. Four species of crabapples are native to North America, and in these the leaves are folded along the midrib in the buds. Sweet crabapple (*Malus coronaria*) is found from New York south just into Georgia and west to Arkansas and north to Illinois and southern Ontario. The prairie crabapple (*Malus ioensis*) is found in the Great Plains from Wisconsin and Minnesota south to central Texas and Louisiana. The southern crabapple (*Malus angustifolia*) is found from Virginia south to Florida and west to Louisiana and Illinois. In the West the Oregon crabapple (*Malus fusca*) has an oblong, not rounded, fruit and is seen from southeastern Alaska to northern California.

Malus develops a domed, leafy crown, rounded in old trees but more conical and spiky in young ones. *Malus domestica*, the orchard apple, has much bigger fruit and is hairy in all its parts.

BARK
Smooth and green-brown with large orange breathing pores (lenticels) in young trees, becoming brown and cracked in old trees.

American basswood

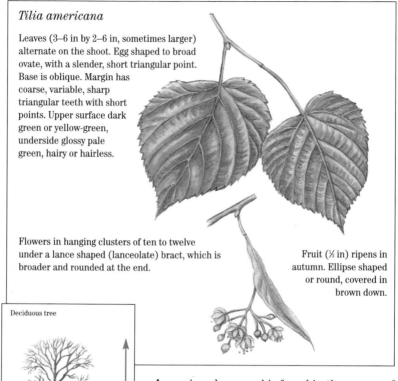

Tilia americana

Leaves (3–6 in by 2–6 in, sometimes larger) alternate on the shoot. Egg shaped to broad ovate, with a slender, short triangular point. Base is oblique. Margin has coarse, variable, sharp triangular teeth with short points. Upper surface dark green or yellow-green, underside glossy pale green, hairy or hairless.

Flowers in hanging clusters of ten to twelve under a lance shaped (lanceolate) bract, which is broader and rounded at the end.

Fruit (⅓ in) ripens in autumn. Ellipse shaped or round, covered in brown down.

Deciduous tree

60–100 ft

American basswood is found in the square of territory from New Brunswick to southeastern Manitoba, south to northeastern Oklahoma and east into North Carolina. It grows on moist soils in valleys or on slopes, where it is found with other hardwood trees. Basswoods or lindens have a characteristic bract, which is attached to the flower cluster and persists in the fruit. The flowers are fragrant and very attractive to bees. The wood is white, with a soft, fine texture. It is easily carved, and it is used for food boxes, furniture and beehives. The common name, basswood, refers to the use of the bark. If beaten to separate the bundles of fibers, these can be woven into rope or into mats. Two other lindens are found in the southeastern U.S.A. White basswood (*Tilia heterophylla*) has leaves covered by a dense layer of white hairs. This gives the tree a distinctive appearance from a distance, when leaves are upturned by a breeze. Carolina basswood (*Tilia caroliniana*) is a smaller tree; the undersides of its leaves have a soft covering of rust-colored hairs.

Tilia americana forms a tall, upright tree with a long crown composed of small and frequently drooping branches. Often there is a ring of sprout shoots at the tree's base.

BARK
Smooth and dark gray in young trees, becoming fissured into narrow, scaly ridges.

Little leaf linden

Tilia cordata

Leaves alternate on the shoot, a rounded egg shape to a triangular egg shape, 1–3 in by 1–3 in. Apex has an abrupt, slender point, base is oblique and deeply heart shaped. Margin has regular, sharp teeth. Upper surface matte and somewhat bluish green, underside bluish with red or orange tufts (axils) in the junction of the veins. Leaf stalk ¼–1 ½ in.

Shoot green and soon without hairs. Buds bluntly pointed, green with only two protective scales showing.

Deciduous tree

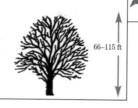

66–115 ft

Flowers fragrant and whitish cream in early summer. Held level, with or above the leaves, in clusters of five to eleven with a large, leafy bract.

Fruit oval to round, smooth, with a thin shell. No ridges.

SIMILAR SPECIES
Tilia platyphyllos
Leaves of large-leaved linden are a broad egg shape and larger than small-leaved linden's, 2 ⅕–6 in by 2 ¾–5 in. They have a dense covering of simple hairs on both surfaces.

Little leaf linden is planted as an ornamental or shade tree from Quebec and Wisconsin south to Virginia, in Nebraska and on the West Coast in British Columbia and Washington. The common name of small-leaved linden is to distinguish it from the large-leaved linden, which is planted in the same regions. Both these trees are native to Europe from Britain and Spain. Both species have been managed in woodlands as coppiced trees—they are cut down to ground level every few years and allowed to sprout. The stumps can be 20 ft across and perhaps 2,000 years old, although in such large stumps the center rots away, leaving an incomplete ring of stems. Coppicing was carried out partly for the wood, but more especially for the bark. This was stripped off the stems and rotted, leaving the fibers, which were twisted into rope.

Small and large-leaved linden have produced a hybrid, *T. europaea*. This is known as common lime, since it is common in cultivation (although rare in the wild). Its leaves are shiny with axillary brown tufts on the underside, and less hairy. The tree produces an excess of basal suckers and honeydew.

Tilia cordata occurs naturally in woodland, but is most often seen as a specimen tree. It can be used for avenues. The crown is rounded, usually taller than broad, unlike the tree shown here.

BARK
Gray and smooth on young trees, becoming darker and fissuring into scaly plates on old trees.

California laurel, Oregon myrtle

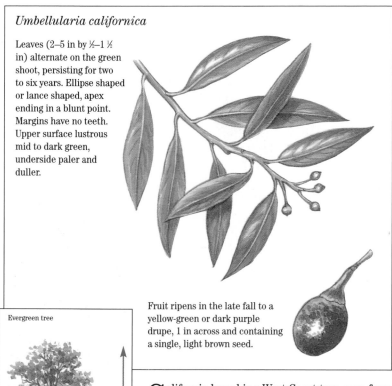

Umbellularia californica

Leaves (2–5 in by ½–1 ½ in) alternate on the green shoot, persisting for two to six years. Ellipse shaped or lance shaped, apex ending in a blunt point. Margins have no teeth. Upper surface lustrous mid to dark green, underside paler and duller.

Fruit ripens in the late fall to a yellow-green or dark purple drupe, 1 in across and containing a single, light brown seed.

Evergreen tree

Up to 80 ft

California laurel is a West Coast tree seen from central Oregon to southern California, primarily in the coastal ranges, but also in the Sierra Nevada. It tolerates a wide range of soils and aspects: its roots spread deep and wide, especially on mountain canyon sites or in mixed, open forest. The best growth is made on moist, valley-bottom sites, where trees to 175 ft in height and single stems up to 12 ft in diameter have been recorded. More usually, it is seen on poorer sites, where mature trees can range from 20 ft upwards, and on several stems.

The foliage is strongly aromatic, with a delightfully appealing scent from the essential oils in the foliage and twigs. Don't inhale much: it can cause splitting headaches, and some cases of unconsciousness are reported. The oils may also cause dermatitis. The common name in the U.K., where it is occasionally cultivated as an amenity tree, is California headache tree. In Oregon, it seems to go by the name Oregon laurel, with Oregon myrtle referring to the lumber. This is dense and hard, shiny, light brown, with a fine texture and is used for high-quality or high-value items, such as furniture.

Umbellularia californica makes a
majestic tree on the best sites,
but is more often seen as an
evergreen with several stems
in mixed forests.

BARK
Thin and dull brown,
becoming gray-brown.
Fissures into tight, scaly
plates on older trees.

Sassafras

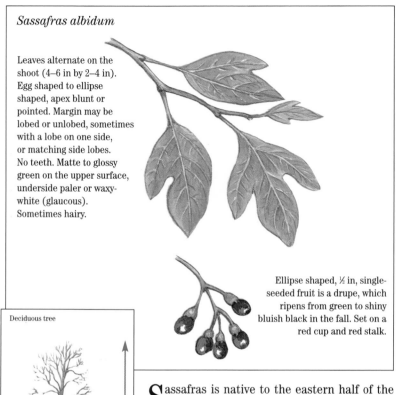

Sassafras albidum

Leaves alternate on the shoot (4–6 in by 2–4 in). Egg shaped to ellipse shaped, apex blunt or pointed. Margin may be lobed or unlobed, sometimes with a lobe on one side, or matching side lobes. No teeth. Matte to glossy green on the upper surface, underside paler or waxy-white (glaucous). Sometimes hairy.

Ellipse shaped, ½ in, single-seeded fruit is a drupe, which ripens from green to shiny bluish black in the fall. Set on a red cup and red stalk.

Deciduous tree

Up to 60 ft, rarely to 100 ft

Sassafras is native to the eastern half of the country, from Maine across to Michigan (just extending into southern Ontario), and from there south to eastern Texas and central Florida. It is a tree of moist, sandy, poor soils and adept at exploiting abandoned land or forest clearings. This is partly because it can throw suckers from the roots: it can invade an opening or spread into ungrazed pasture, as well as germinate from the seeds, which are widely spread by birds. It is generally only a low tree, often forming the understory in forests.

Sassafras has aromatic foliage, as is indicated by its membership in the mainly tropical or subtropical laurel family. The bark of the roots is distilled into 'oil of sassafras,' used to perfume soap. Sassafras tea is made from the roots, which were once also used to flavor root beer. The twigs and leaf stalks have a spicy, gummy taste if chewed. An extract is used in dental poultices.

Sassafras flowers in spring before the leaves appear, usually with male and female flowers on separate trees. The flowers are yellow-green, with a sweet, lemon scent. The autumn color is yellow, orange or red.

Sassafras albidum forms a dense
egg shaped crown, with short,
stout branches. It is often
surrounded by suckers.

BARK
Gray-brown and
deeply furrowed into
narrow ridges.

Mountain silverbell

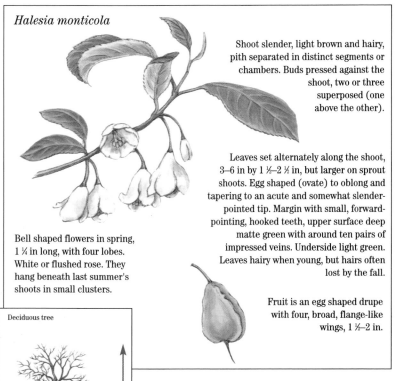

Halesia monticola

Shoot slender, light brown and hairy, pith separated in distinct segments or chambers. Buds pressed against the shoot, two or three superposed (one above the other).

Leaves set alternately along the shoot, 3–6 in by 1 ½–2 ½ in, but larger on sprout shoots. Egg shaped (ovate) to oblong and tapering to an acute and somewhat slender-pointed tip. Margin with small, forward-pointing, hooked teeth, upper surface deep matte green with around ten pairs of impressed veins. Underside light green. Leaves hairy when young, but hairs often lost by the fall.

Bell shaped flowers in spring, 1 ¼ in long, with four lobes. White or flushed rose. They hang beneath last summer's shoots in small clusters.

Fruit is an egg shaped drupe with four, broad, flange-like wings, 1 ½–2 in.

Deciduous tree

Up to 80 ft

Mountain silverbell is found from North Carolina to Arkansas and Oklahoma. It grows in hardwood forests, especially on moist soils along streams and valley floors, but always at altitudes above the 3,000 ft contour. Silverbells are characterized by small, star-shaped hairs which cover all the parts. These are not easily seen by the naked eye, although they can be felt—they make the shoots and leaves feel rough. The hairs have several short arms radiating out from the base. These are a characteristic of the Styrax family, to which *Halesia* belongs. They are also seen in the basswoods (page 182) and some of the oaks. Mountain silverbell is closely allied to Carolina silverbell, *Halesia caroliniana*, and often included in this species. However, Carolina silverbell makes a smaller tree, usually less than 30 ft, with smaller flowers, only ¾ in long. Its bark is tight, with small pressed-down scales. Two other species of silverbell occur in the South east. Two-wing silverbell, *Halesia diptera*, has fruits with only two wings and also only grows to around 30 ft. Little silverbell, *Halesia parviflora*, is rarely taller than 25 ft, and has a club-like fruit with four narrow wings.

Halesia monticola has a column shaped or broad, cone shaped crown, which in old trees becomes rounded. It is particularly attractive in May when festooned with its hanging, bell shaped flowers.

BARK
Light brown to gray in young trees, with deep orange or pink fissures. In old trees it becomes darker gray, and splits into loose plates.

Flowering dogwood

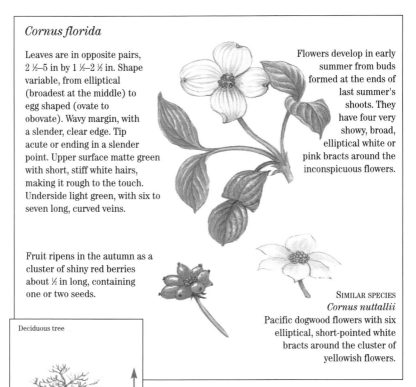

Cornus florida

Leaves are in opposite pairs, 2 ½–5 in by 1 ½–2 ½ in. Shape variable, from elliptical (broadest at the middle) to egg shaped (ovate to obovate). Wavy margin, with a slender, clear edge. Tip acute or ending in a slender point. Upper surface matte green with short, stiff white hairs, making it rough to the touch. Underside light green, with six to seven long, curved veins.

Flowers develop in early summer from buds formed at the ends of last summer's shoots. They have four very showy, broad, elliptical white or pink bracts around the inconspicuous flowers.

Fruit ripens in the autumn as a cluster of shiny red berries about ½ in long, containing one or two seeds.

SIMILAR SPECIES
Cornus nuttallii
Pacific dogwood flowers with six elliptical, short-pointed white bracts around the cluster of yellowish flowers.

Deciduous tree

Up to 30 ft

Flowering dogwood is found in the East from Maine to southern Ontario and south to Florida and eastern Texas, where it is an understory component of hardwood forests. It grows on both dry and moist sites, and from sea level to almost 5,000 ft in the southern Appalachians.

The tree's showy display is not, in fact, created by the flowers, which are small, with yellow petals, clustered together in heads of about ½ in across; it is, in fact, the bracts, which surround the flower heads, forming a protective 'bud' over the flowers from their formation in autumn through the winter. In spring, as growth starts, the bracts expand and color, usually white, but in some forms pink. The fruits are in clusters, potentially one fruit from each of the flowers, but in practice only some are fertilized.

Pacific dogwood, is found along the West Coast from southeastern British Columbia to southern California. In the north it is close to the coast, but in California it is seen in the Sierra Nevada. It makes a majestic tree, especially when in flower. The flowers are much larger than flowering dogwood's.

Cornus florida makes a
flamboyant tree when in flower,
and the dying foliage is an
attractive red color in fall.

BARK
Reddish-brown; breaks
into small, square plates.

Sourwood, sorrel tree

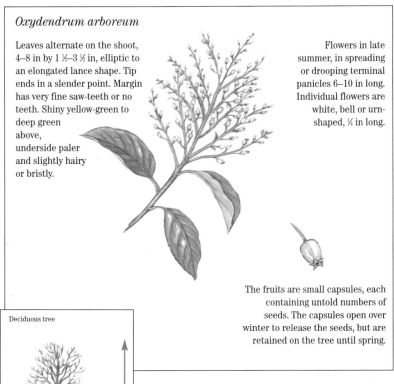

Oxydendrum arboreum

Leaves alternate on the shoot, 4–8 in by 1 ½–3 ½ in, elliptic to an elongated lance shape. Tip ends in a slender point. Margin has very fine saw-teeth or no teeth. Shiny yellow-green to deep green above, underside paler and slightly hairy or bristly.

Flowers in late summer, in spreading or drooping terminal panicles 6–10 in long. Individual flowers are white, bell or urn-shaped, ¼ in long.

The fruits are small capsules, each containing untold numbers of seeds. The capsules open over winter to release the seeds, but are retained on the tree until spring.

Deciduous tree

20–50 ft

Sourwood comes from the eastern states, from Pennsylvania and Maryland south to northern Florida and west to Louisiana and southern Indiana. It is an understory tree in valley and upland sites, growing with pines and oaks. It makes its best growth in the southern Appalachians, such as the Great Smoky Mountains National Park, where it is found up to 5,000 ft. It is also known as the lily of the valley tree, a reference to the similarity of the flowers to those of the bulb of the same name, sharing both the bulb's flower shape and fragrance. Sourwood is, however, a member of the heather family, along with madrone (*Arbutus*) page 198, with which it also shares small bell shaped flowers. However, unlike this genus, it will not grow on limey sites, requiring a well-drained, acidic soil. The common and generic names refer to the taste of the foliage, which is pleasantly acidic. The tree takes on brilliant red colors in the fall, often before the flowers have lost all their color—so it provides color from mid summer onwards, when many other trees are past their spring exuberance. The red-brown wood is hard and heavy.

Oxydendrum arboreum flowers in mid to late summer before turning red or scarlet in autumn. It forms a narrow, conical or rounded tree, especially when in woodland conditions.

BARK
Brown or gray; thick, fissuring into scaly ridges.

Olive

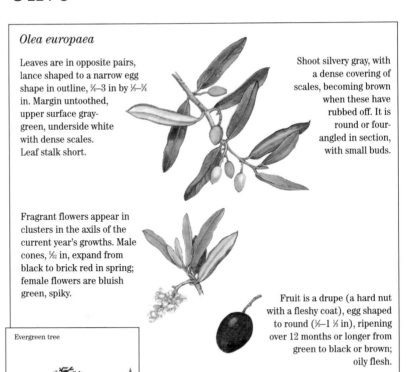

Olea europaea

Leaves are in opposite pairs, lance shaped to a narrow egg shape in outline, ¾–3 in by ⅕–¾ in. Margin untoothed, upper surface gray-green, underside white with dense scales. Leaf stalk short.

Shoot silvery gray, with a dense covering of scales, becoming brown when these have rubbed off. It is round or four-angled in section, with small buds.

Fragrant flowers appear in clusters in the axils of the current year's growths. Male cones, ⁵⁄₃₂ in, expand from black to brick red in spring; female flowers are bluish green, spiky.

Fruit is a drupe (a hard nut with a fleshy coat), egg shaped to round (⅖–1 ⅕ in), ripening over 12 months or longer from green to black or brown; oily flesh.

Evergreen tree

33 ft, occasionally taller

This tree is so characteristic of the Mediterranean landscape that it would be natural to assume that it is a native of the region. In fact, it is more likely to have been introduced at an early stage from the Arabian peninsula, where it seems to be native in the dry, barren mountains between Saudi Arabia and Yemen. Wild olives are found here in apparently natural settings: they have smaller leaves than planted ones, and spiny shoots. The tree cannot tolerate more than a few degrees of frost, and like other plants which thrive in hot places, it does not put up with shade. It is very tolerant of drought once established, ideally suited to the wet winters/dry hot summers of the Mediterranean climate.

The olive tree is important worldwide as the source of olive oil, which is pressed from the fleshy covering of the fruit, and considered the best of the vegetable oils, containing many polyunsaturates. These are said to be better for the body than other types of fat, but nonetheless still seem to add to one's girth. The wood is black or brown. It polishes well and is used for small items or joinery, or for flooring and paneling. In California it is a popular 'landscape' tree.

Olea europaea are often pollarded
when raised in groves. This
simplifies fruit collection—and
makes for small, dense crowns
on stout boles.

BARK
Silvery gray, becoming
finely fissured and fluted,
with crossing ridges that
give deep, dark hollows.

Madrone

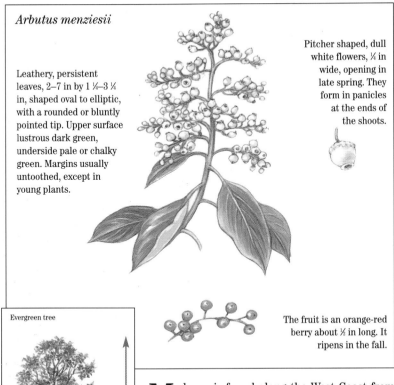

Arbutus menziesii

Leathery, persistent leaves, 2–7 in by 1 ¼–3 ¼ in, shaped oval to elliptic, with a rounded or bluntly pointed tip. Upper surface lustrous dark green, underside pale or chalky green. Margins usually untoothed, except in young plants.

Pitcher shaped, dull white flowers, ¼ in wide, opening in late spring. They form in panicles at the ends of the shoots.

Evergreen tree

33–82 ft

The fruit is an orange-red berry about ½ in long. It ripens in the fall.

Madrone is found along the West Coast from southern British Columbia to California, where it also occurs in the Sierra Nevada and on Santa Cruz Island. It is a species of canyons and uplands, occurring from sea level up to 5,000 feet, mainly in oak and conifer forest where there is a seasonal dry period. The flowers make a fair show in spring, and are followed by the even more showy fruits in autumn. The foliage is glossy and evergreen, making it a neat tree at all seasons. However, the most stunning display is the bark. At the base of old trees is dark purple or red-brown bark, cracking into small squares. On the branches, after the tree is four years old, the bark peels to reveal new, smooth, orange bark, which in turn ages red or yellow-pink, before peeling again. This procession of color makes it one of the most attractive barks of any tree, a spectacular sight on a well-grown specimen in middle age. The fruits are like small strawberries, and contain a number of small seeds set in the flesh. They are edible but can cause stomach cramps if eaten in quantity. The flowers yield honey, while the wood is hard and used to make small, durable items, such as weavers' shuttles.

Arbutus menziesii makes an upright, evergreen tree with glossy foliage.

BARK
Peels in large, papery, thin red sheets, except at the base, where it cracks into small squares.

Eastern redbud

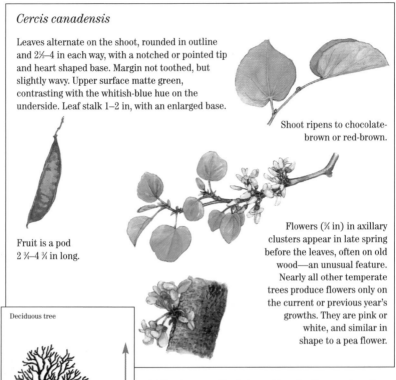

Cercis canadensis

Leaves alternate on the shoot, rounded in outline and 2½–4 in each way, with a notched or pointed tip and heart shaped base. Margin not toothed, but slightly wavy. Upper surface matte green, contrasting with the whitish-blue hue on the underside. Leaf stalk 1–2 in, with an enlarged base.

Shoot ripens to chocolate-brown or red-brown.

Fruit is a pod
2 ¾–4 ¾ in long.

Flowers (¾ in) in axillary clusters appear in late spring before the leaves, often on old wood—an unusual feature. Nearly all other temperate trees produce flowers only on the current or previous year's growths. They are pink or white, and similar in shape to a pea flower.

Deciduous tree

26–49 ft

astern redbud is native to the region from New Jersey south to central Florida and as far west as southeast Nebraska and Texas. It also occurs over the border in northern Mexico. It is a tree of moist valley soils, and is planted as an ornamental. It is most frequently seen as a shrub, but scattered small to medium trees occur throughout the range. However, even here it is usually encountered on several stems, not with a single stout bole. Eastern redbud belongs to the legume family, as is shown by the fruit being a pod like a pea or bean. Unusually for this family, the leaves are simple, whereas most legumes have leaves composed of many separate leaflets—see Kentucky coffee tree (page 260). Another way in which it is unusual is in showy flowers. They are the typical 'pea' flower, but are carried not just on the wood formed last summer but often on the old branches or trunks—similar to how honey locust thorns grow out of older trunks. The flowers make a delightful display in April or May before the leaves expand. The timber is hard and tough, red overall, but with beautifully dark veins: prized in joinery.

Cercis canadensis makes a fine display in late spring when the twigs and often the main branches are wreathed with the flowers. The trunk often leans, putting the rounded crown off center.

BARK
Gray-brown, smooth, cracking into small brown squares.

Orange

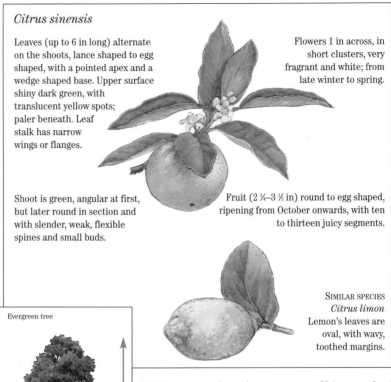

Citrus sinensis

Leaves (up to 6 in long) alternate on the shoots, lance shaped to egg shaped, with a pointed apex and a wedge shaped base. Upper surface shiny dark green, with translucent yellow spots; paler beneath. Leaf stalk has narrow wings or flanges.

Flowers 1 in across, in short clusters, very fragrant and white; from late winter to spring.

Shoot is green, angular at first, but later round in section and with slender, weak, flexible spines and small buds.

Fruit (2 ¾–3 ½ in) round to egg shaped, ripening from October onwards, with ten to thirteen juicy segments.

SIMILAR SPECIES
Citrus limon
Lemon's leaves are oval, with wavy, toothed margins.

Evergreen tree

Up to 33 ft, but usually smaller

The orange is native to eastern China south of the River Yangtze or 'Golden Sands river', but of course has been widely cultivated in Florida and California for a very long time. It was probably introduced to Europe before Roman times. The fruit, known as a 'hesperid', is unique to the genus *Citrus*. It consists of eight to fifteen segments surrounded by a whitish pith and a zest or outer skin which contains many gland cells. The seeds are carried in the segments. The juicy bits of the segments are believed to derive from enlarged hair cells. The leaves are also unusual in being jointed between the leaf stalk and the blade; and the stalk often has wings or flanges which function as part of the leaf area. Indeed in some species of orange the winged stalk has nearly the same area as the leaf blade; in fact, the grapefruit is one of these.

The lemon has a similar long history of cultivation to the orange, and is believed to have come from southeastern China. The acid flesh and the characteristic shape are sure means of identification. When in flower, lemon can be separated by its 25 to 40 stamens, compared to only 20 in the orange.

Citrus sinensis cultivated in groves are rarely allowed to grow more than 10 feet in height because this simplifies harvesting. The bushes may carry fruits and flowers at the same time.

BARK
Gray, smooth or wrinkled.

Cider gum

Eucalyptus gunnii

Green or waxy blue-green juvenile leaves in opposite pairs. They are broad oval to rounded, 1–1 ¾ in by ¾–1 ½ in; no stalk.

Leathery, green or bluish, waxy adult leaves, the same on both sides and alternate on the pink-purple waxy shoot. They hang down, lance shaped to egg shaped, 2 ½–4 in by 1–1 ½ in, with a pointed tip and rounded to wedge shaped base. Stalk is wrinkled.

Fruit is a woody capsule (⅜ in) shaped like a spinning top, ripening in summer after flowering.

White, fluffy flowers in clusters of three, in mid summer.

Evergreen tree

SIMILAR SPECIES
Eucalyptus niphophila
Snow gum has lance shaped leaves 2 ½–4 in long with an abruptly hooked tip. The flowers and fruits are in clusters of seven or more.

66–98 ft

Cider gum is native to Tasmania and southeastern mainland Australia. It is one of the hardiest of the many species of eucalypts and is cultivated in the warmer parts of North America. The name eucalyptus literally means 'fused petals'. These are not showy and large as in most flowers. Instead, they form a cap over the developing flower bud which, in due course, falls off as the flower opens. The other unusual feature of eucalypts is the foliage. Most trees have two types of leaves: seed leaves (the first pair of leaves produced as the seed germinates), and adult leaves. Eucalypts produce seed, juvenile and adult leaves, and intermediates. Juvenile leaves (see above) give way to the adult leaves, which have stalks and are similar on both sides. When a eucalypt is cut back, the first leaves it makes are juvenile ones, however old the tree. The strongly clustered and colored juvenile leaves are favored by flower arrangers.

Snow gum is native to southeastern mainland Australia. It is generally a small tree, reaching only 33 ft. Its main attraction is the snow-white color of the newly exposed bark.

The tree's new shoots have only a few small leaves, giving a halo effect over the denser crown of a fast growing tree. Young trees are very narrow and upright, but they become rounded as they mature.

BARK
At first pale green or cream colored beneath, but gradually changing to gray before being shed in large sheets.

Blue gum eucalyptus

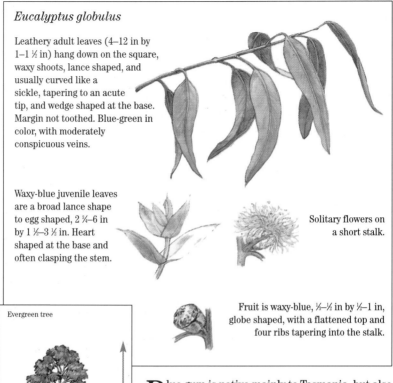

Eucalyptus globulus

Leathery adult leaves (4–12 in by 1–1 ½ in) hang down on the square, waxy shoots, lance shaped, and usually curved like a sickle, tapering to an acute tip, and wedge shaped at the base. Margin not toothed. Blue-green in color, with moderately conspicuous veins.

Waxy-blue juvenile leaves are a broad lance shape to egg shaped, 2 ¾–6 in by 1 ½–3 ½ in. Heart shaped at the base and often clasping the stem.

Solitary flowers on a short stalk.

Fruit is waxy-blue, ⅛–½ in by ½–1 in, globe shaped, with a flattened top and four ribs tapering into the stalk.

Evergreen tree

33–148 ft

Blue gum is native mainly to Tasmania, but also to a single area in Victoria on the mainland of southeastern Australia. It is probably the most widely cultivated of the eucalypts, growing well in climates which are not cold in winter.

Blue gum eucalyptus was introduced to San Francisco in 1875 and since then has naturalized into the hills to the south. It also grows in southern Oregon along the coast. Further spread is restricted by winter cold. However, it is grown in areas where it is not hardy in summer bedding schemes for its blue foliage, growing 6 to 10 feet by fall.

Blue gum eucalyptus is unique amongst the six hundred or so eucalypts in having single flowers and fruits. Eleven other species have between three and fifteen flowers in a cluster. The fruits are larger, distinctively ribbed and warty.

Blue gum eucalyptus is planted as a timber tree, especially for pulp. The trees are harvested every few years and make sprout shoots which grow vigorously from the stump without need for replanting.

As a young tree, *Eucalyptus globulus* has a very narrow crown with a single trunk. In the open (as here) it develops a rounded crown.

BARK
This is shed to show white beneath, which gradually matures through fawn, pink and gray to gray-brown before shedding once more.

Cucumber tree

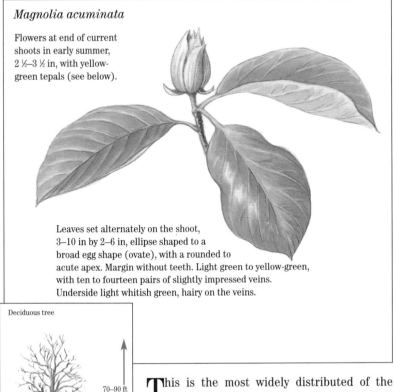

Magnolia acuminata

Flowers at end of current
shoots in early summer,
2 ½–3 ½ in, with yellow-
green tepals (see below).

Leaves set alternately on the shoot,
3–10 in by 2–6 in, ellipse shaped to a
broad egg shape (ovate), with a rounded to
acute apex. Margin without teeth. Light green to yellow-green,
with ten to fourteen pairs of slightly impressed veins.
Underside light whitish green, hairy on the veins.

Deciduous tree

70–90 ft

This is the most widely distributed of the *Magnolia* species. It occurs from New York just into southern Ontario and across to Missouri, and from there to Louisiana and Florida. It grows on slopes and in ravines, along streams and generally on base-rich soils. The common name is derived from the fruit, which resembles a small cucumber, which although often green, matures to a shocking pink or red in color. The seeds have a fleshy scarlet coat and when the fruit opens, they hang by silky threads. Displayed in this way, they await a passing bird to eat them, pass them through its digestive system and deposit them, where, with luck, the seed can germinate.

The flowers appear after the new foliage, and so are buried from sight except if viewed from above. This is also true of the other seven *Magnolia* species native to the eastern half of the continent. By contrast, many of the Asian *Magnolias* carry their flowers on the bare boughs before the leaves expand, and for this reason are highly prized by gardeners. Of these saucer magnolia, *Magnolia soulangeana*, is the most widely cultivated.

Magnolia acuminata develops a strong upright trunk with a crown composed of short spreading or ascending branches.

BARK
Smooth and brown or gray-brown in young trees, developing narrow, scaly, forking fissures and ridges in older trees.

Southern magnolia

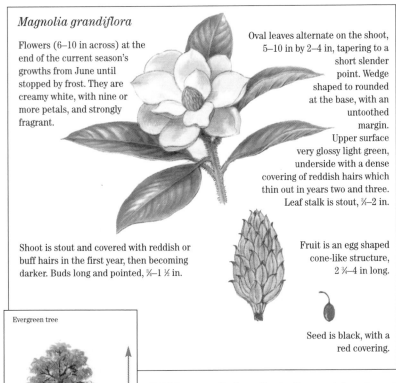

Magnolia grandiflora

Flowers (6–10 in across) at the end of the current season's growths from June until stopped by frost. They are creamy white, with nine or more petals, and strongly fragrant.

Oval leaves alternate on the shoot, 5–10 in by 2–4 in, tapering to a short slender point. Wedge shaped to rounded at the base, with an untoothed margin. Upper surface very glossy light green, underside with a dense covering of reddish hairs which thin out in years two and three. Leaf stalk is stout, ¾–2 in.

Shoot is stout and covered with reddish or buff hairs in the first year, then becoming darker. Buds long and pointed, ¾–1 ½ in.

Fruit is an egg shaped cone-like structure, 2 ¾–4 in long.

Seed is black, with a red covering.

Evergreen tree

33–50 ft

This magnolia is native to the coastal regions of southeastern U.S.A. from North Carolina south to Florida along the Atlantic coast and along the Gulf of Mexico coast to Texas. It occurs in moist lowland valley sites where it is associated with other broadleaved tree species and is much hardier than you might expect, given its southern origin. The tree is grown for its combination of glossy leaves and large flowers. It has been cultivated in Britain and Western Europe for centuries and has produced a number of cultivars. These vary in leaf size and shape, and in the density of the reddish or rufous hairs on the leaf underside (an attractive feature). In fact, they are all useful ornamental trees because they produce deliciously scented blooms in succession through the summer. Examples include 'Exmouth', which has narrow leaves and makes a more upright tree; and 'Goliath', with suitably sized (12 ft) blooms. The scientific name refers to the large flowers: when named, it had the largest of any known species. The tree is also known as bull bay—'bull' referring to the glossy foliage, vaguely similar to that of bay laurel, but much larger.

Magnolia grandiflora has an upright crown with the lower branches slightly drooping. It is often grown beside walls, but will also do well as a freestanding tree.

BARK
Light brown, becoming rough and scaly at the base.

Tulip tree

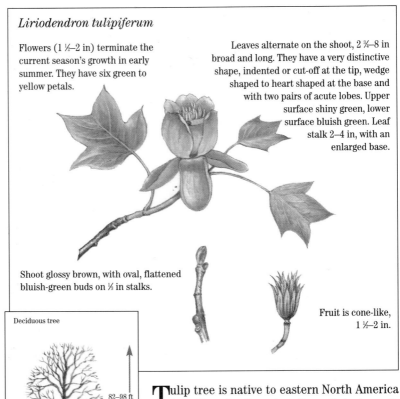

Liriodendron tulipiferum

Flowers (1 ½–2 in) terminate the current season's growth in early summer. They have six green to yellow petals.

Leaves alternate on the shoot, 2 ¾–8 in broad and long. They have a very distinctive shape, indented or cut-off at the tip, wedge shaped to heart shaped at the base and with two pairs of acute lobes. Upper surface shiny green, lower surface bluish green. Leaf stalk 2–4 in, with an enlarged base.

Shoot glossy brown, with oval, flattened bluish-green buds on ⅓ in stalks.

Fruit is cone-like, 1 ½–2 in.

Deciduous tree

82–98 ft

Tulip tree is native to eastern North America from Nova Scotia and southern Ontario south to Florida and Louisiana. Within this range, it occurs on well-drained but moist lowland valley sites, where it can reach upwards of 148 ft. The name tulip tree refers to the appearance of the flower. These are quite attractive in detail, but often hidden by the foliage. It is also known as yellow poplar, after its appearance during the autumn, when it goes yellow-gold. It is also planted for the pale yellow timber: of moderate quality, it is used for furniture and is resistant to woodworm. Tulip tree is an example of the close relationship between the flora of eastern North America and China. The genus contains only two species. The other, *Liriodendron chinense*, is native from eastern China south into Vietnam. Its leaves generally have a narrower waist between the middle pairs of lobes and are a more waxy-blue beneath.

Tulip tree is planted as an ornamental and can make interesting avenues. However, unless named clones are used, trees raised from seed tend to be too variable to make neat rows.

Young *liriodendron tulipiferum* have a neat column shape, but as they get older they develop a more rounded habit, without low branches. This means that the flowers are often out of reach of the ground.

BARK
Gray-brown or gray; smooth on young trees, becoming gray or silvery-gray, with platy scales at the base and orange-brown fissures.

American holly

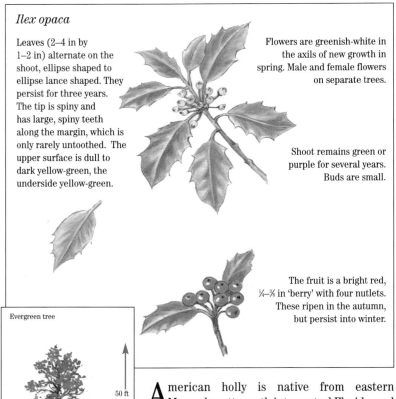

Ilex opaca

Leaves (2–4 in by 1–2 in) alternate on the shoot, ellipse shaped to ellipse lance shaped. They persist for three years. The tip is spiny and has large, spiny teeth along the margin, which is only rarely untoothed. The upper surface is dull to dark yellow-green, the underside yellow-green.

Flowers are greenish-white in the axils of new growth in spring. Male and female flowers on separate trees.

Shoot remains green or purple for several years. Buds are small.

The fruit is a bright red, ¼–⅜ in 'berry' with four nutlets. These ripen in the autumn, but persist into winter.

Evergreen tree

50 ft

American holly is native from eastern Massachusetts south into central Florida, and west to southeastern Missouri and central Texas. It grows on floodplains and moist soils as a component of hardwood forests. The wood is white, with a fine texture that takes stains or polish.

More than 1,000 cultivar have been named. Especially popular are those with bright foliage, yellow fruits, or leaves edged with creamy white.

English holly, *Ilex aquifolium*, is seen in New England, where it is not fully hardy, and on the West Coast. It has a more lustrous foliage than *Ilex opaca*, and is more attractive as a landscape tree. Its flowers, and thus its fruits, are borne on last year's shoots. The leaves are similarly spiny. Several native species of holly sometimes make small trees. Among them Dahoon, *Ilex cassine*, grows to about 30 ft in the Southeast from North Carolina south to Florida and west to Louisiana, mainly on swampy sites. It has evergreen, shiny, dark green leaves which are oblong to egg shaped (obovate) and usually without teeth or spines on the margin.

Ilex opaca develops a narrow but dense crown, conical in young trees but more rounded, with irregular branching, in old trees.

BARK
Gray-white. It may be smooth, or roughened by warty growths.

Southern catalpa

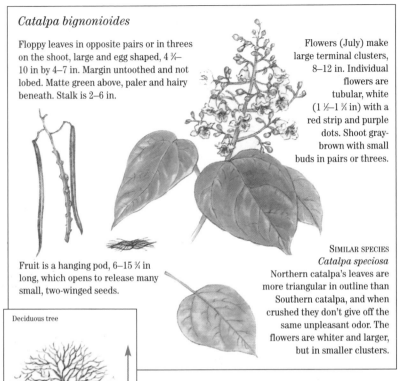

Catalpa bignonioides

Floppy leaves in opposite pairs or in threes on the shoot, large and egg shaped, 4 ¾–10 in by 4–7 in. Margin untoothed and not lobed. Matte green above, paler and hairy beneath. Stalk is 2–6 in.

Flowers (July) make large terminal clusters, 8–12 in. Individual flowers are tubular, white (1 ½–1 ¾ in) with a red strip and purple dots. Shoot gray-brown with small buds in pairs or threes.

Fruit is a hanging pod, 6–15 ¾ in long, which opens to release many small, two-winged seeds.

SIMILAR SPECIES
Catalpa speciosa
Northern catalpa's leaves are more triangular in outline than Southern catalpa, and when crushed they don't give off the same unpleasant odor. The flowers are whiter and larger, but in smaller clusters.

Deciduous tree

33 ft, rarely up to 49 ft

Southern catalpa is native to southeastern U.S.A. from Georgia and Florida west to Alabama and Mississippi, where it occurs at the margins of woods. It has been widely planted outside this native range, and despite its southerly origin it is hardy. With most broadleaved trees, the crown diameter of a tree grown in the open is roughly equal to its height, but this is one of the exceptions where the crown is much broader than tall. The fruits hang down from the old flower trusses like strands of spaghetti. The leaves are thin, easily tattered by the wind, and stay green into the autumn until killed by frost. If crushed, they give off an unpleasant odor. The genus name, *Catalpa*, is the Native American word for the tree, while the flowers are similar to the tropical climber *Bignonia*. Its timber is tough and durable, but coarse-grained.

Northern catalpa is a native of central U.S.A. along the Mississippi valley from Arkansas to Indiana. It makes a more tree-like tree, growing to 33 or 66 ft, and has a more conventional width than Southern catalpa. With its northern origin, it has a greater tolerance to cold winters.

Catalpa bignonioides is a glorious sight in July when laden with the large clusters of flowers, but is a dead loss in autumn when the leaves fall without turning any color except black. The large leaves are thin, and cast only a light shade.

BARK
Pink and brown. Smooth in young trees, developing thin, gray scaly flakes on older trees.

217

Royal paulownia or Empress tree

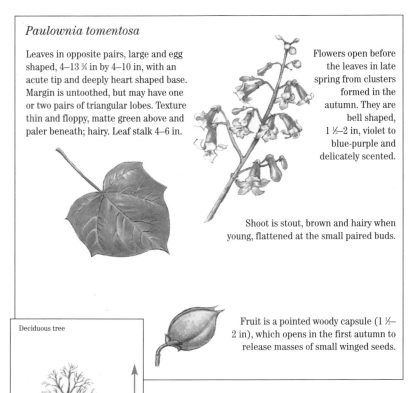

Paulownia tomentosa

Leaves in opposite pairs, large and egg shaped, 4–13 ¾ in by 4–10 in, with an acute tip and deeply heart shaped base. Margin is untoothed, but may have one or two pairs of triangular lobes. Texture thin and floppy, matte green above and paler beneath; hairy. Leaf stalk 4–6 in.

Flowers open before the leaves in late spring from clusters formed in the autumn. They are bell shaped, 1 ½–2 in, violet to blue-purple and delicately scented.

Shoot is stout, brown and hairy when young, flattened at the small paired buds.

Deciduous tree

33–66 ft

Fruit is a pointed woody capsule (1 ½– 2 in), which opens in the first autumn to release masses of small winged seeds.

Paulownia is native to northern China, but was an early introduction to Japan and taken from there to the Eastern U.S.A. in 1834. It is a fast-grower. The current season's shoots are pithy. If not cut back before autumn frost arrives, they quickly thicken and produce the fine-grained timber used for delicate implements such as chopsticks. The tree casts only a light shade and is used in agro-forestry as a canopy tree, allowing crops to grow below. It is planted as an ornamental and is naturalized throughout the East, from southern New England, south. It can also be grown as a shrub, and if cut down in spring it will produce a shoot 6 ½ to 10 ft in length, with leaves 24 in across. The flowers can be damaged by spring frosts, while the leaves fall in autumn at the first hint of cold weather. The genus name is after Princess Anna Paulovna, a daughter of Tsar Paul the First of Russia. It is similar to *Catalpa* (page 216), but the two genera are usually placed in different families. Nonetheless, they are both considered to be close to the ancestral tree from which both families have evolved.

To be fully appreciated, the flowers of this spreading tree need to be seen either against a dark background, or from above. It quickly forms a tall, domed crown.

BARK
Smooth, gray or purple; developing gray lines as it matures.

Sycamore

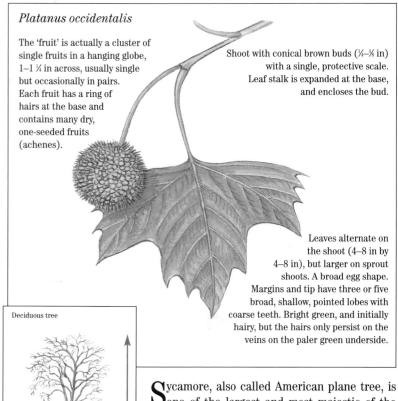

Platanus occidentalis

The 'fruit' is actually a cluster of single fruits in a hanging globe, 1–1 ¼ in across, usually single but occasionally in pairs. Each fruit has a ring of hairs at the base and contains many dry, one-seeded fruits (achenes).

Shoot with conical brown buds (¼–⅜ in) with a single, protective scale. Leaf stalk is expanded at the base, and encloses the bud.

Leaves alternate on the shoot (4–8 in by 4–8 in), but larger on sprout shoots. A broad egg shape. Margins and tip have three or five broad, shallow, pointed lobes with coarse teeth. Bright green, and initially hairy, but the hairs only persist on the veins on the paler green underside.

Deciduous tree

60–100 ft, occasionally 150 ft

Sycamore, also called American plane tree, is one of the largest and most majestic of the Eastern hardwoods. It is found from southwestern Maine south to northern Florida, west across southern Ontario to eastern Nebraska and then south through southern Texas into northeast Mexico. It grows on moist sites, along lakes and rivers, and in swamps and floodplains. However, it also seeds on abandoned fields or on mine spoil. It needs moisture at the time of germination, but once established it will grow on much drier sites. This is widely planted as a shade tree: it has large, dense leaves and tolerates smoke and atmospheric pollution. The heartwood is light red-brown, fairly hard and heavy. It is resistant to splitting, which made it suitable for shaping into buttons—the lumber is still known as buttonwood. Other uses include paneling, flooring and odd items such as butcher blocks. In the Southwest are two related species, Arizona sycamore (*Platanus wightii*) seen in Arizona, New Mexico and Mexico; and California sycamore (*Platanus racemosa*) seen in California and Baja California. These bear three to seven fruits along a stalk, and have deeply lobed leaves.

Platanus occidentalis has a long, straight trunk with heavy, spreading branches forming a broad, open crown.

BARK
Smooth and white except at the very base of large trees where it becomes furrowed and dark brown. Becomes mottled and darker as it peels in thin flakes to reveal white beneath.

London plane

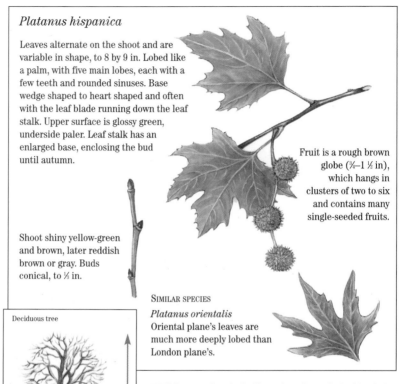

Platanus hispanica

Leaves alternate on the shoot and are variable in shape, to 8 by 9 in. Lobed like a palm, with five main lobes, each with a few teeth and rounded sinuses. Base wedge shaped to heart shaped and often with the leaf blade running down the leaf stalk. Upper surface is glossy green, underside paler. Leaf stalk has an enlarged base, enclosing the bud until autumn.

Fruit is a rough brown globe (¾–1 ½ in), which hangs in clusters of two to six and contains many single-seeded fruits.

Shoot shiny yellow-green and brown, later reddish brown or gray. Buds conical, to ⅕ in.

SIMILAR SPECIES
Platanus orientalis
Oriental plane's leaves are much more deeply lobed than London plane's.

Deciduous tree

66–131 ft

This species is believed to be a hybrid of the oriental plane (see below) and the sycamore from North America, the latter giving it more shallowly lobed leaves than oriental plane's. It has hybrid vigor and quickly makes a large tree. The seeds are fertile and give rise to seedlings combining the characteristics of the original two species, and a confusing array of forms. It tolerates urban conditions, including atmospheric pollution and excessive pruning, and will grow well on a range of soils. The leaves adopt russet colors in autumn. They are very slow to decompose. The hairs on the new leaves can cause allergic reactions in some people. The timber is of good quality, used for paneling. The tree was for a long time known as *Platanus acerifolia*, from the resemblance of the leaves to certain maples, such as sycamore maple (*Acer pseudoplatanus*, page 226) and Norway maple (*Acer platanoides*, page 228).

Oriental plane comes from Greece, Bulgaria, Cyprus and Turkey, and possibly from farther east in Asia. It is a tree of valley bottoms, where it grows in moist but well-drained river gravels, which allows it to survive hot summers.

Platanus hispanica is associated with the squares and parks of London and other major cities, where it makes a large tree capable of complementing the architecture.

BARK
Smooth, shedding in large plates, especially in autumn, to reveal a creamy white which slowly darkens to brown. At the base of old trees, the bark is thicker and scaly, and does not shed.

Sweetgum

Liquidambar styraciflua

Leaves alternate on the shoot, 2 ¾–6 in by 3 ½–6 ¾ in, with five, rarely seven, oblong to egg shaped lobes which are pointed at the tip and separated by deep, acute spaces (sinuses). Margin has small, rounded, hooked teeth. Upper side matte green, indented along the veins, underside paler, and shiny. Stalk 2–6 in, with the bottom part (³⁄₁₆–⅓ in) thickened.

Shoot matures to green-brown or gray-brown, with pointed, shiny green (³⁄₁₆ in) buds.

The fruit hangs in a round cluster, 1 in in diameter, containing many beaked capsules which open to release one or two black winged seeds.

Deciduous tree

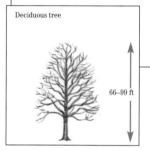

66–99 ft

This tree is a native of eastern U.S.A., where it occurs from Connecticut across to Illinois and south to Florida and Texas. It is also native to northern and eastern Mexico. The trees from the southern part of its range can be evergreen in mild climates, and generally get their deep autumn color late. The names (genus, scientific and common) refer to the resin, which can be extracted from the bark. This is used to perfume hides in tanneries and was once used as a chewing gum. The leaves have a resinous scent when crushed. The original source of the resin was the oriental liquidambar, *L. orientalis*, a smaller tree from western and southwestern Turkey, and Rhodes. The genus *Liquidambar* is superficially very similar to several maples, such as sycamore (page 220). However, it can always be separated from the maples by looking at the shoot: on liquidambar, the leaves and buds are arranged alternately along the shoot in a helix, whereas in the maples they are in opposite pairs. It is much closer to plane (page 222), but easily distinguished by the toothed leaf margins and the scaly bark. The base of the leaf stalk does not hide the bud.

Liquidambar styraciflua is used as a large specimen tree and is particularly attractive in autumn when the dying leaves turn scarlet or red. Young trees (as seen here) are column or cone shaped; old trees have tall, domed crowns.

BARK
Gray, often with weak corky wings when young, becoming rough on old trees, with narrow scaly ridges.

Sycamore maple

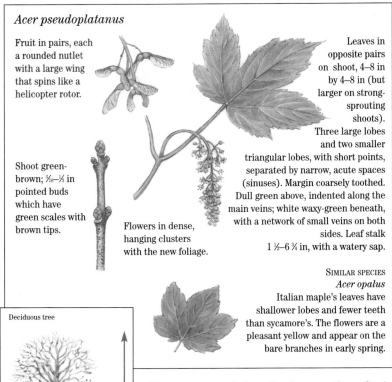

Acer pseudoplatanus

Fruit in pairs, each a rounded nutlet with a large wing that spins like a helicopter rotor.

Shoot green-brown; 3/16–1/3 in pointed buds which have green scales with brown tips.

Flowers in dense, hanging clusters with the new foliage.

Leaves in opposite pairs on shoot, 4–8 in by 4–8 in (but larger on strong-sprouting shoots). Three large lobes and two smaller triangular lobes, with short points, separated by narrow, acute spaces (sinuses). Margin coarsely toothed. Dull green above, indented along the main veins; white waxy-green beneath, with a network of small veins on both sides. Leaf stalk 1 1/2–6 3/4 in, with a watery sap.

SIMILAR SPECIES
Acer opalus
Italian maple's leaves have shallower lobes and fewer teeth than sycamore's. The flowers are a pleasant yellow and appear on the bare branches in early spring.

Deciduous tree

49–115 ft

Sycamore maple is native from northern Spain in the west to southern Germany; also eastwards across Central and Southern Europe into northern Turkey, and the Caucasus as far as the Caspian Sea. It is grown as a shade tree across the United States. The winged seeds help to spread the tree far and wide on the wind. A seed produces two large seed leaves (or cotyledons), then normal leaves. As the seeds favor freshly dug soil, they thrive in gardens, to the irritation of gardeners. Sycamore is a very tough tree, tolerating poor, exposed sites, and urban abuse. The foliage is usually covered in tar spots, caused by a fungus, and only occasionally achieves a moderate yellow autumn color. The high-quality wood is used for paneling and violins.

Italian maple, a rarity in North America, is native to southern and eastern Spain, southeastern France, southern Switzerland, the Balkans, Italy and North Africa. Its foliage is very similar to sycamore's but easily separated when it flowers in spring: the flowers and fruits are in smaller clusters.

Mature *Acer pseudoplatanus* develops a majestic domed crown, but before this the tree goes through a prolonged stage when the crown is conical and spiky.

BARK
Smooth and silver-gray or brown, becoming more and more cracked as the tree ages. Eventually, it has peeling scales, 4–8 in by 2–4 in.

Norway maple

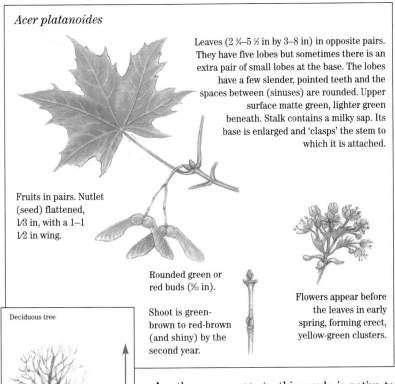

Acer platanoides

Leaves (2 ¾–5 ½ in by 3–8 in) in opposite pairs. They have five lobes but sometimes there is an extra pair of small lobes at the base. The lobes have a few slender, pointed teeth and the spaces between (sinuses) are rounded. Upper surface matte green, lighter green beneath. Stalk contains a milky sap. Its base is enlarged and 'clasps' the stem to which it is attached.

Fruits in pairs. Nutlet (seed) flattened, 1/3 in, with a 1–1 1/2 in wing.

Rounded green or red buds (3/32 in).

Deciduous tree

49–82 ft

Shoot is green-brown to red-brown (and shiny) by the second year.

Flowers appear before the leaves in early spring, forming erect, yellow-green clusters.

As the name suggests, this maple is native to Norway—actually to the southeast of the country. However, its range extends to southern Sweden and east into Russia; also south to the Balkans, central Italy and northern Spain. In France it is native in the east; it is not native to Britain.

Norway maple is planted as a street and shade tree across the U.S.A., and has become naturalized; sometimes to excess. The leaves are similar to sugar maple, sycamore maple, London plane and sycamore (plane), but can be separated by the milky sap in the leaf stalk, whereas these other trees have a watery sap.

Norway maple has given rise to a number of cultivars, especially ones with purple foliage. The best of these (because the purple is transient, replaced by more natural green foliage) is 'Shwedleri', but more common are forms such as 'Crimson King' and 'Goldsworth's Purple', in which the bright purple of spring becomes dull and dank in summer before being lightened by the autumn color. All the purple forms also have purple bracts with the yellow flowers and are respectable at that stage.

Acer platanoides makes a domed tree which is particularly attractive when carrying the flowers in early spring. Seen here is a young tree in autumn color with a typical spiky crown. The tree is planted as an ornamental and is tolerant of poor urban conditions.

BARK
Gray or pinkish-brown gray, smooth on young trees, then becoming folded. Old trees develop shallow fissures and ridges.

Field maple

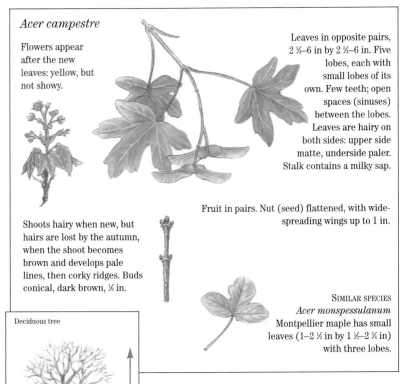

Acer campestre

Flowers appear after the new leaves: yellow, but not showy.

Leaves in opposite pairs, 2 ¾–6 in by 2 ¾–6 in. Five lobes, each with small lobes of its own. Few teeth; open spaces (sinuses) between the lobes. Leaves are hairy on both sides: upper side matte, underside paler. Stalk contains a milky sap.

Fruit in pairs. Nut (seed) flattened, with wide-spreading wings up to 1 in.

Shoots hairy when new, but hairs are lost by the autumn, when the shoot becomes brown and develops pale lines, then corky ridges. Buds conical, dark brown, ⅛ in.

SIMILAR SPECIES
Acer monspessulanum
Montpellier maple has small leaves (1–2 ⅛ in by 1 ½–2 ¾ in) with three lobes.

Deciduous tree

Usually 32–40 ft, but up to 49–82 ft

Field maple is widely planted across the U.S.A. as a small tree in landscape schemes. It is the best maple for dry alkaline sites. It is native to England and Wales, south into Spain and across southern Europe to Turkey and the Caucasus; also to a small area in North Africa. The tree has a durable reddish wood suitable for turnery, but not available in large sizes. As with other maples, the foliage has been used for animal fodder. These days, the species is quite popular as an ornamental, because of its attractive yellow autumn color. It grows on a wide range of sites. Field maple can be used to make hedges and withstands clipping. The new growth following clipping is often purple or pink for a few days, adding to the color of a trimmed hedgerow.

Montpellier maple is uncommon in the U.S.A. but is native to southern Europe, east into Turkey and the Caucasus; also to North Africa. It is adapted to hot climates. Although the tree has some similarity with field maple, it is not closely related. The sap in the leaf stalk is watery, not milky. *Monspessulanum* is the Latin name for Montpellier in southern France.

Acer campestre is typical of hedgerows rather than woods. It is often seen as a multi-stemmed tree, but can be drawn up to a height if sheltered by other trees.

BARK
Gray-brown and pale, becoming darker on old trees and developing small scaly squares or flakes.

Sugar maple

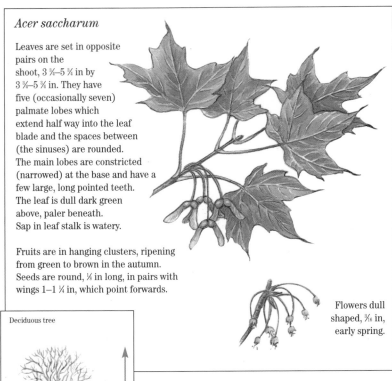

Acer saccharum

Leaves are set in opposite pairs on the shoot, 3 ¾–5 ¼ in by 3 ¾–5 ¼ in. They have five (occasionally seven) palmate lobes which extend half way into the leaf blade and the spaces between (the sinuses) are rounded. The main lobes are constricted (narrowed) at the base and have a few large, long pointed teeth. The leaf is dull dark green above, paler beneath. Sap in leaf stalk is watery.

Fruits are in hanging clusters, ripening from green to brown in the autumn. Seeds are round, ¼ in long, in pairs with wings 1–1 ¼ in, which point forwards.

Flowers dull shaped, ³⁄₁₆ in, early spring.

Deciduous tree

60–80 ft

Sugar maple is found from the Atlantic coast to southeastern Manitoba and south to northern Georgia and South Carolina, where it favors moist upland soils and valleys. It is perhaps best known for providing the most outstanding show of color in the New England fall.

The tree is the principal source of maple syrup. The sap of all trees contains sugars which are transported from the leaves to the roots, both to feed the roots and also to store energy. In spring, the sap moves the stored sugars back to the shoots to power the spring growth spurt. In sugar maple, the proportion of sugars in the sap is greater than in other trees: about one part in forty (2.5 percent). Native Americans learned to tap sugar maple for this sap, but had no way of preserving it. The first colonists, with their iron pans, managed to do so by boiling the sap, concentrating the sugar content. About 25 to 35 gallons of sap are needed to make a gallon of maple syrup, with a sugar content of some 60–65 percent. Sugar maple also makes high-quality, hard timber, used for furniture, veneers, floors and general lumber.

Acer saccharum makes a dense tree with a broad, rounded crown. It turns a rich gold or red in the fall.

BARK
Dark gray and furrowed into long, scaly plates in old trees. In young trees it is smooth.

Japanese maple

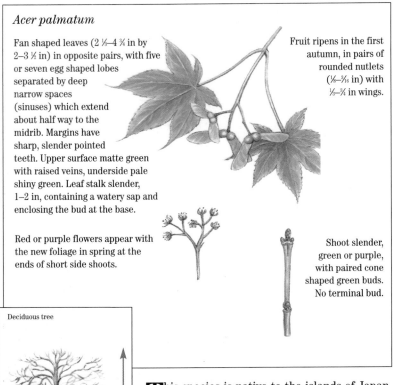

Acer palmatum

Fan shaped leaves (2 ⅛–4 ¾ in by 2–3 ½ in) in opposite pairs, with five or seven egg shaped lobes separated by deep narrow spaces (sinuses) which extend about half way to the midrib. Margins have sharp, slender pointed teeth. Upper surface matte green with raised veins, underside pale shiny green. Leaf stalk slender, 1–2 in, containing a watery sap and enclosing the bud at the base.

Fruit ripens in the first autumn, in pairs of rounded nutlets (⅛–¾₆ in) with ⅓–¾ in wings.

Red or purple flowers appear with the new foliage in spring at the ends of short side shoots.

Shoot slender, green or purple, with paired cone shaped green buds. No terminal bud.

Deciduous tree

20–33 ft

This species is native to the islands of Japan, where it is mainly found in the mountains. It is also native to the mainland of Asia in Korea, and northeastern and central China. It is a popular garden ornamental, boasting brilliant autumn colors: red, orange or clear yellow. The Japanese have valued it for centuries and selected many forms. These include forms with cut or dissected leaves, forms with purple leaves, normal green-leaved forms and dwarf forms with curious leaves. The cut-leaved forms make shrubs rather than trees. The purple-leaved selections with normal leaves make small trees. The purple color is produced by an excess of the pigment xanthocyanin, which masks the normal green. Xanthocyanin is produced by most broadleaved trees, but normally only in the new foliage; purple-leaved forms are selected to keep a higher proportion of the pigment. However, the amount of pigment retained varies, and in most purple-leaved forms the foliage becomes a dull purple-green over the summer, only reviving with the autumn color. Some selections, such as 'Bloodgood', named after the nursery it originated from, stay more purple than others.

Acer palmatum makes a leafy, rounded crown. Although generally small, and by nature an understory tree (as shown here), it can grow up to 49 ft in sheltered, moist sites.

BARK
Gray-green, smooth with strips on young trees. On older trees it is gray or gray-brown and slightly fissured.

Red maple

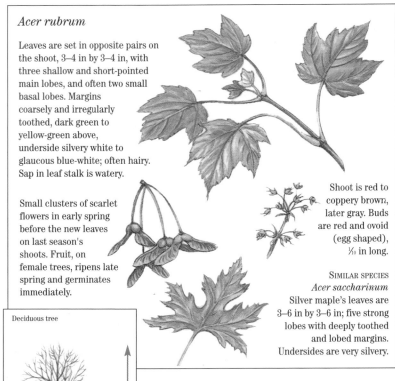

Acer rubrum

Leaves are set in opposite pairs on the shoot, 3–4 in by 3–4 in, with three shallow and short-pointed main lobes, and often two small basal lobes. Margins coarsely and irregularly toothed, dark green to yellow-green above, underside silvery white to glaucous blue-white; often hairy. Sap in leaf stalk is watery.

Small clusters of scarlet flowers in early spring before the new leaves on last season's shoots. Fruit, on female trees, ripens late spring and germinates immediately.

Deciduous tree

60–80 ft

Shoot is red to coppery brown, later gray. Buds are red and ovoid (egg shaped), $\frac{1}{10}$ in long.

SIMILAR SPECIES
Acer saccharinum
Silver maple's leaves are 3–6 in by 3–6 in; five strong lobes with deeply toothed and lobed margins. Undersides are very silvery.

Red maple is native to the eastern side of the continent from Newfoundland west to Ontario and south to eastern Texas and Florida. It is the most widely distributed eastern tree. Common on wet or moist river bottom sites and in mixed hardwood forest, less often on dry ridges.

Red maple matures its seeds in late spring, releasing them when the soil is still moist, but not flooded; they germinate quickly. The tree is aptly named, as the flowers have reddish petals and the shoots are similarly colored in the first winter. However, red maple is mainly noticed for its brilliant red hues, displayed by the dying leaves in the fall, which make a major contribution to the autumn gaiety of the eastern states.

Silver maple has a similar distribution to red maple, except it is absent from the coastal plain and does not extend into eastern Texas. It is restricted to wet sites and also ripens its seeds in late spring. Like red maple, it is fast-growing, and widely cultivated as an ornamental. The branches are rather brittle and it is prone to wind damage.

Acer rubrum makes a tall tree, usually with an upright and rather narrow crown, assuming brilliant red colors in the fall.

BARK
Silvery gray or gray, smooth in young trees, but in old trees becoming cracked into long, lifting plates.

237

Rowan tree

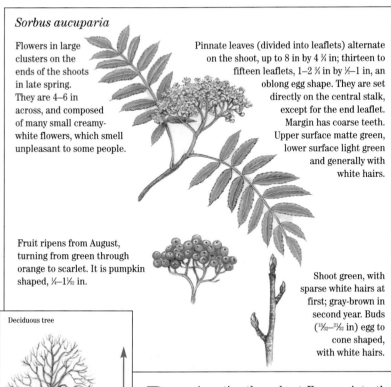

Sorbus aucuparia

Flowers in large clusters on the ends of the shoots in late spring. They are 4–6 in across, and composed of many small creamy-white flowers, which smell unpleasant to some people.

Pinnate leaves (divided into leaflets) alternate on the shoot, up to 8 in by 4 ¾ in; thirteen to fifteen leaflets, 1–2 ¾ in by ½–1 in, an oblong egg shape. They are set directly on the central stalk, except for the end leaflet. Margin has coarse teeth. Upper surface matte green, lower surface light green and generally with white hairs.

Fruit ripens from August, turning from green through orange to scarlet. It is pumpkin shaped, ¼–1½₂ in.

Shoot green, with sparse white hairs at first; gray-brown in second year. Buds (¹³⁄₃₂–²¹⁄₃₂ in) egg to cone shaped, with white hairs.

Deciduous tree

26–33 ft

Rowan is native throughout Europe, into the Caucasus and south into North Africa's Atlas Mountains. It is planted as an ornamental tree and has become naturalized in North America from southeastern Alaska across southern Canada and from Maine to Minnesota and in California. American mountain ash (*Sorbus americana*) is native to the Northeast from Newfoundland south to northern Georgia and west to Illinois and north to western Ontario. It differs in the long, pointed, lance-shaped leaflets, which have saw-teeth and are soon hairless. The fruits are ¼ in across. Showy mountain ash, *Sorus decora*, occurs over this same area, although not extending down the Appalachians, and being found farther north into Labrador. It has oval to oblong sharply pointed leaflets which are blue-green along the upper surface. The fruits are larger, ⅜–½ in across. The name, rowan, is probably derived from the Norse name for the tree. Rowan is planted as an ornamental tree in parks, gardens and streets. The fruits are attractive to birds and small mammals, and usually stripped from the trees before autumn. As with other species in the apple family, these contain cyanide.

Sorbus aucuparia is characteristic of parks and gardens in the U.S.A. but also occurs in lowland broadleaved and conifer forest. It has an upright, rather conical habit, but older trees are more rounded.

BARK
Smooth shiny gray or silvery gray, becoming browner on old trees and forming scaly ridges at the base.

Manna ash or flowering ash

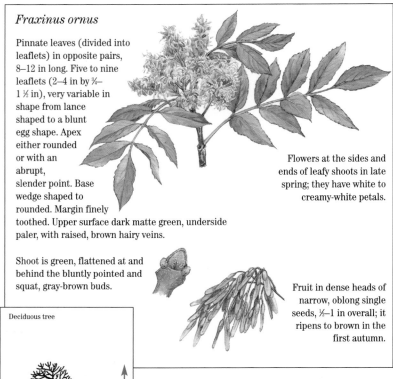

Fraxinus ornus

Pinnate leaves (divided into leaflets) in opposite pairs, 8–12 in long. Five to nine leaflets (2–4 in by ¾– 1 ½ in), very variable in shape from lance shaped to a blunt egg shape. Apex either rounded or with an abrupt, slender point. Base wedge shaped to rounded. Margin finely toothed. Upper surface dark matte green, underside paler, with raised, brown hairy veins.

Shoot is green, flattened at and behind the bluntly pointed and squat, gray-brown buds.

Flowers at the sides and ends of leafy shoots in late spring; they have white to creamy-white petals.

Fruit in dense heads of narrow, oblong single seeds, ½–1 in overall; it ripens to brown in the first autumn.

Deciduous tree

49–82 ft

Manna ash, planted as a flowering or shade tree, is native to southeastern Europe and around the Mediterranean and Black Sea coasts of western Turkey: an area of hot, dry summers and wet winters. It belongs to a small section of the ash genus which has petals in the flowers. By any standard, it is attractive in flower, but, compared with green and white ashes, it is outstanding and fully deserves its alternative common name, flowering ash. The gray-brown buds, rounded, but ending in a point, provide an easy way to separate it from ash and narrow-leaved ash all year.

Manna ash can be tapped to produce a sugar: slits are made in the bark of young trees; sap runs out and congeals on exposure to air. It is very sweet. One of the sugars it contains is mannitol, commonly used as a mild laxative. There is probably no truth in the legend that the sap was the manna which nourished the Israelites in the Sinai Desert: the tree does not grow there. The timber is similar to that of other ashes, and used for the same purposes.

Fraxinus ornus makes a showy tree in May when laden with the creamy-white flowers. Both old and young trees have domed crowns.

BARK
Dark gray and smooth, developing weak fissures at the base.

Green ash, red ash

Fraxinus pennsylvanica
Pinnate leaves in opposite pairs on the shoot, up to 10 in long. Leaflets 2–5 in by 1–1 ½ in, with the larger ones towards the apex. Usually seven, but often five or nine. Egg shaped, tapering to a slender tip. No stalk at the base. Upper surface matte green, with hairs on ten or so pairs of dimpled veins; underside gray-green.

Fruit 1 ¼–2 ½ in long, in clusters, each nutlet with an egg shaped (obovate) wing which extends or has two flanges along the sides of the nutlet.

Shoot olive-brown, maturing to gray, either with soft down, or without hairs at all. Buds golden brown, ⅜ in.

SIMILAR SPECIES
Fraxinus americana
Leaves up to 14 in long with five to nine leaflets, which are 2 ½–6 in by ¹⁵⁄₃₂–3 in. Oblong-lanceolate, tapering to a pointed apex, and are set on a ⅛ in stalk. Whitish-green underside.

Deciduous tree

Up to 60 ft

Green ash occurs in the wild from Nova Scotia west to Alberta, and south to eastern Texas and Florida. It is native to the moist alluvial soils along rivers and streams, where it is fast growing but shallow rooted. It does not tolerate shade, but will grow on drier and better drained sites. Valued for the shade it provides, it is also grown in shelterbelts in the Midwest, and on land reclamation sites.

The tree is very variable in the degree of hairiness displayed by its leaves and shoots. While red ash is very hairy, green ash (var. *lanceolata*) is the least hairy. However, botanically, this is considered a minor distinction.

American ash has a similarly wide distribution, but does not extend west of Ontario. It grows on moist but well-drained soils, such as on steep valley slopes and along river valleys. It is more tolerant of shade than green ash. The wings of the fruit do not run more than halfway along the nutlet. It gives good early fall color, varying from a pleasing yellow to intense purple or maroon. The wood of both of these ashes is hard and heavy and used for baseball bats and oars.

Fraxinus pennsylvanica develops a dense, rounded or irregular crown which is bright green during summer and turns yellow in autumn.

BARK
Bark gray-brown with shallow reddish fissures. In mature trees it becomes scaly with a reddish inner layer.

Butternut

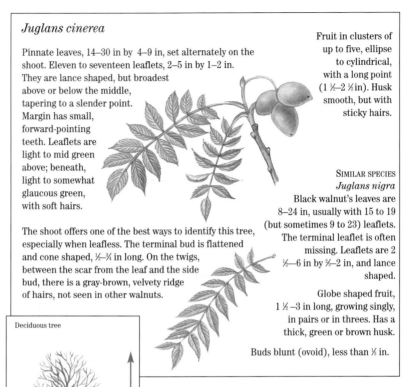

Juglans cinerea

Pinnate leaves, 14–30 in by 4–9 in, set alternately on the shoot. Eleven to seventeen leaflets, 2–5 in by 1–2 in. They are lance shaped, but broadest above or below the middle, tapering to a slender point. Margin has small, forward-pointing teeth. Leaflets are light to mid green above; beneath, light to somewhat glaucous green, with soft hairs.

The shoot offers one of the best ways to identify this tree, especially when leafless. The terminal bud is flattened and cone shaped, ½–¾ in long. On the twigs, between the scar from the leaf and the side bud, there is a gray-brown, velvety ridge of hairs, not seen in other walnuts.

Fruit in clusters of up to five, ellipse to cylindrical, with a long point (1 ½–2 ½ in). Husk smooth, but with sticky hairs.

SIMILAR SPECIES
Juglans nigra
Black walnut's leaves are 8–24 in, usually with 15 to 19 (but sometimes 9 to 23) leaflets. The terminal leaflet is often missing. Leaflets are 2 ½–6 in by ¾–2 in, and lance shaped.

Globe shaped fruit, 1 ½ –3 in long, growing singly, in pairs or in threes. Has a thick, green or brown husk.

Buds blunt (ovoid), less than ⅛ in.

Deciduous tree

Up to 60 ft

Butternut is found from Minnesota to Quebec, east to New Brunswick and south to Georgia and Arkansas. It grows along river terraces and valley bottoms, also on dry rocky slopes in association with other hardwoods. A disease, butternut canker, is killing the species right across its range, which is shrinking because the tree does not resprout from the base. Butternut seeds have a very oily kernel, which makes them palatable, but also likely to deteriorate if not properly stored. The husk will stain the fingers yellow or brown.

Walnuts (*Juglans*) differ from hickories (*Carya*) (see page 246) in several ways. The pith running along the center of the twigs is separated into small chambers; the male catkins are single; and the husk around the fruit does not split to release the seed. Walnut wood is not as strong as hickory, but produces beautifully figured veneers, and has long been used in cabinet making. Black walnut has a similar distribution, growing on moist, well-drained sites in mixed forests. It is longer-lived and taller.

Juglans cinerea has a short trunk with a broad, open crown on stout, ascending branches.

BARK
Light gray or grayish brown, with shallow fissures and smooth or scaly plates.

Bitternut hickory

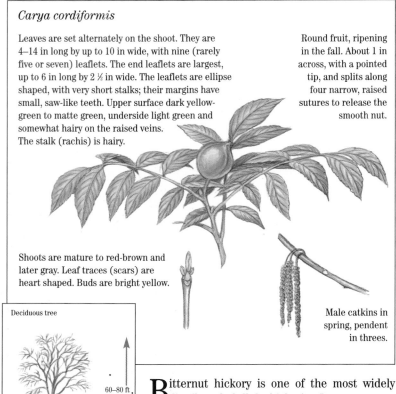

Carya cordiformis

Leaves are set alternately on the shoot. They are 4–14 in long by up to 10 in wide, with nine (rarely five or seven) leaflets. The end leaflets are largest, up to 6 in long by 2 ½ in wide. The leaflets are ellipse shaped, with very short stalks; their margins have small, saw-like teeth. Upper surface dark yellow-green to matte green, underside light green and somewhat hairy on the raised veins. The stalk (rachis) is hairy.

Round fruit, ripening in the fall. About 1 in across, with a pointed tip, and splits along four narrow, raised sutures to release the smooth nut.

Shoots are mature to red-brown and later gray. Leaf traces (scars) are heart shaped. Buds are bright yellow.

Deciduous tree

60–80 ft

Male catkins in spring, pendent in threes.

Bitternut hickory is one of the most widely distributed of all the hickories. It occurs across a great swath of the eastern U.S.A., from New Hampshire to Minnesota and south to eastern Texas, also occurring just inside the northern Florida Panhandle. It also just makes it into the southern part of Quebec and Ontario. In the south of its range, it is mainly found on valley bottoms, but to the north it also occurs on drier upland sites. It grows in mixed hardwood forests. The most useful distinguishing character of this tree is its sulfur-yellow buds on the ripe winter shoots. The bud scales are valvate, with little or no overlap between opposing scales, whereas in most hickories the bud scales are imbricate, that is, pressed down on top of one another. The nut (used by the early settlers to make lamp oil) has a bitter kernel: probably desirable from the tree's point of view. The wood is useful for flooring, furniture, tool handles and baseball bats. Hickories are members of the walnut family, but differ from the walnut genus *Juglans* in several ways. The key difference is the pith in the center of the shoot, which is solid in hickory and separated into chambers in walnut.

Carya cordiformis makes a tall tree with a broad, rounded crown.

BARK
Grayish light brown, with shallow furrows and narrow, scaly, forking ridges.

Shagbark hickory

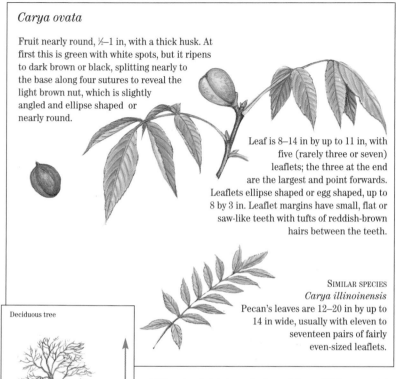

Carya ovata

Fruit nearly round, ½–1 in, with a thick husk. At first this is green with white spots, but it ripens to dark brown or black, splitting nearly to the base along four sutures to reveal the light brown nut, which is slightly angled and ellipse shaped or nearly round.

Leaf is 8–14 in by up to 11 in, with five (rarely three or seven) leaflets; the three at the end are the largest and point forwards. Leaflets ellipse shaped or egg shaped, up to 8 by 3 in. Leaflet margins have small, flat or saw-like teeth with tufts of reddish-brown hairs between the teeth.

SIMILAR SPECIES
Carya illinoinensis
Pecan's leaves are 12–20 in by up to 14 in wide, usually with eleven to seventeen pairs of fairly even-sized leaflets.

Deciduous tree

66–98 ft

Shagbark hickory is found from Maine west to Quebec and southeastern Minnesota; also south to southeastern Texas and Georgia, with a variety in northeastern Mexico. It prefers moist valley and upland sites, and grows in mixed hardwood forests. The large leaves (with five leaflets, the end trio pointing forwards) are distinctive—but so too is the bark, which gives the tree its common name. In older trees, it forms into large, thin plates, 20-24 in long. These peel away from the trunk at both ends, before eventually falling. However, the bark on young trees, in their first twenty-five years or so, is simply rough and shaggy, without the characteristic plates. The fruit of shagbark is sweet and oily. Native Americans used to soak the kernels in boiling water and pound them to make a milky paste, used in cooking.

Pecan is the hickory with the best-tasting fruit. It is native to the territory between Iowa, Indiana, Louisiana and Texas, and also south into northeastern Mexico. However, it has been extensively planted and is the principal nut tree of American origin. In the wild, it is found on well-drained but moist valley sites.

248

Carya illinoinensis, illustrated here, makes a rounded crown when young, developing into a spreading crown when mature. *Carya ovata* is similar but develops a narrow, irregular crown on a long trunk, turning golden brown in autumn.

BARK
Pale gray. Develops long plates or scales which curl away at both ends before falling.

Tree of heaven

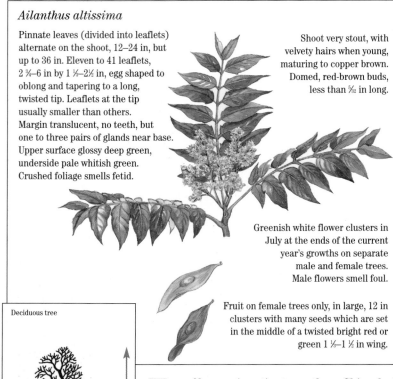

Ailanthus altissima

Pinnate leaves (divided into leaflets) alternate on the shoot, 12–24 in, but up to 36 in. Eleven to 41 leaflets, 2 ¾–6 in by 1 ¼–2½ in, egg shaped to oblong and tapering to a long, twisted tip. Leaflets at the tip usually smaller than others. Margin translucent, no teeth, but one to three pairs of glands near base. Upper surface glossy deep green, underside pale whitish green. Crushed foliage smells fetid.

Shoot very stout, with velvety hairs when young, maturing to copper brown. Domed, red-brown buds, less than ⁵⁄₃₂ in long.

Greenish white flower clusters in July at the ends of the current year's growths on separate male and female trees. Male flowers smell foul.

Fruit on female trees only, in large, 12 in clusters with many seeds which are set in the middle of a twisted bright red or green 1 ¼–1 ½ in wing.

Deciduous tree

49–98 ft

Tree of heaven is native to northern China, but historically cultivated in cities across North America and is now extensively naturalized. It tolerates poor soils and polluted atmosphere and can be attractive when in fruit, especially if the tree has bright red wings to the seeds. It will sucker from the root. The branches are somewhat brittle. The wood is soft and used for pulp.

The genus *Ailanthus*, consisting of some half dozen species, is native from India and China south through southeastern Asia to Australia. Both tree of heaven's common and scientific names have their origin in the Moluccan name for the species, which translates either as 'very tall' or 'reaching the heavens'. The leaves have glands on the margin near the base. These are extrafloral nectaries, that is, nectaries which are not part of the flowers. Their purpose is to make sugary secretions (nectar), which are harvested by ants. In return, the ants keep caterpillars and other leaf-eating insects away from the leaves. The leaves, shoots and flowers, especially the male flowers, have an unpleasant fetid odor, although usually these are above nose level.

Ailanthus altissima makes a rounded crown on a long bole, with bold foliage. It was planted as an ornamental in parks, streets and public gardens and is now extensively naturalized.

BARK
Smooth, gray-brown to dark brown, with white streaks on young trees, developing shallow buff or gray fissures.

251

Box elder

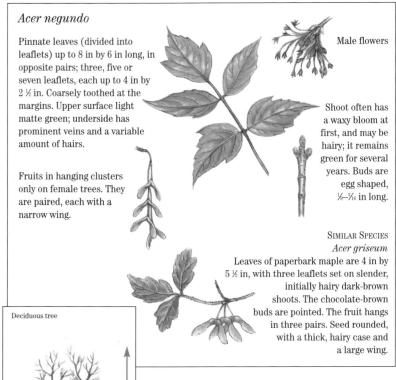

Acer negundo

Pinnate leaves (divided into leaflets) up to 8 in by 6 in long, in opposite pairs; three, five or seven leaflets, each up to 4 in by 2 ½ in. Coarsely toothed at the margins. Upper surface light matte green; underside has prominent veins and a variable amount of hairs.

Fruits in hanging clusters only on female trees. They are paired, each with a narrow wing.

Male flowers

Shoot often has a waxy bloom at first, and may be hairy; it remains green for several years. Buds are egg shaped, ⅛–³⁄₁₆ in long.

SIMILAR SPECIES
Acer griseum
Leaves of paperbark maple are 4 in by 5 ½ in, with three leaflets set on slender, initially hairy dark-brown shoots. The chocolate-brown buds are pointed. The fruit hangs in three pairs. Seed rounded, with a thick, hairy case and a large wing.

Deciduous tree

33–49 ft

Box elder is native to North America from the Atlantic coast to California. It is neither a box (*Buxus* species are shrubs or, rarely, small trees) or an elder. It is, in fact, a maple and is also known as ash-leaved maple, a slightly more descriptive name. During spring it has fifteen minutes of glory when the flowers, especially on male trees, hang attractively beneath the leafless boughs. Otherwise, it is rather uninspiring. There are several variegated forms, which can look attractive as shrubs.

Paperbark maple is native to central China. It makes a wonderful small tree, usually 20 to 26 ft in height, but occasionally taller if located on a sheltered, fertile site. The bark is red-brown, copper or chestnut and peels in paper-thin sheets to reveal a bloomed orange color beneath. It starts peeling on trunks and branches after they are three or four years old, at which point the color extends up into the crown. In autumn, the leaves turn brilliant crimson, red and orange: a display equal to the best. There are inconspicuous yellow flowers. The tree thrives on a wide range of sites, but is slow growing.

Acer negundo usually makes a small, flat-topped tree with spreading branches. Illustrated here is a variegated tree.

BARK
Gray-brown and smooth, becoming darker, with shallow fissures and cracks.

253

Black locust

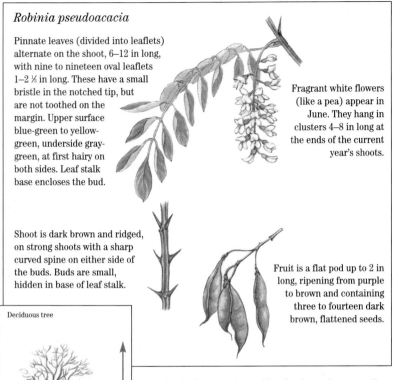

Robinia pseudoacacia

Pinnate leaves (divided into leaflets) alternate on the shoot, 6–12 in long, with nine to nineteen oval leaflets 1–2 ⅙ in long. These have a small bristle in the notched tip, but are not toothed on the margin. Upper surface blue-green to yellow-green, underside gray-green, at first hairy on both sides. Leaf stalk base encloses the bud.

Fragrant white flowers (like a pea) appear in June. They hang in clusters 4–8 in long at the ends of the current year's shoots.

Shoot is dark brown and ridged, on strong shoots with a sharp curved spine on either side of the buds. Buds are small, hidden in base of leaf stalk.

Fruit is a flat pod up to 2 in long, ripening from purple to brown and containing three to fourteen dark brown, flattened seeds.

Deciduous tree

49–82 ft

Black locust is a North American native, occurring naturally in a triangle from Pennsylvania to Ohio and Alabama; also in a separate band from southern Missouri to eastern Oklahoma. It thrives on light sandy soils, but also grows on heavier soils, provided the site is well drained. It has become naturalized in regions with a warm summer climate.

The tree produces root suckers which are usually armed with pairs of sharp spines at each bud or leaf. They are a striking feature, produced only on the vigorous growths and derived from the pair of small primitive leaves or stipules which are found beside the leaves in many broadleaved trees. Stipules tend to be found on the young shoots of species such as *Betula*, *Carpinus* and *Tilia*, and are quickly lost.

Black locust is also known as false acacia, from the scientific name. Black locust is a member of the legume family, whose roots harbor bacteria which can make nitrogen fertilizer for the tree from air in the soil. The timber is of reasonable quality.

Robinia pseudoacacia quickly makes a large, rugged tree with a tall, domed crown, but is rarely as old as its appearance suggests.

BARK
Smooth and brown on young trees, but quickly becoming rough and dark gray, with coarse ridges and furrows.

Japanese pagoda tree

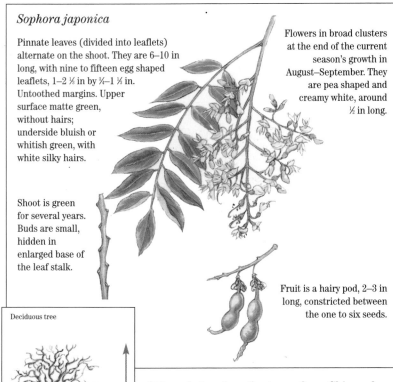

Sophora japonica

Pinnate leaves (divided into leaflets) alternate on the shoot. They are 6–10 in long, with nine to fifteen egg shaped leaflets, 1–2 ⅛ in by ¾–1 ⅛ in. Untoothed margins. Upper surface matte green, without hairs; underside bluish or whitish green, with white silky hairs.

Shoot is green for several years. Buds are small, hidden in enlarged base of the leaf stalk.

Flowers in broad clusters at the end of the current season's growth in August–September. They are pea shaped and creamy white, around ½ in long.

Fruit is a hairy pod, 2–3 in long, constricted between the one to six seeds.

Deciduous tree

49–82 ft

Pagoda tree is native to northern China, where it is one of the few large broadleaved trees that can cope with the local dry winters and springs. It is possibly also a native of Japan, but the evidence suggests that it was probably introduced there when Japan embraced Buddhism. It was introduced to North America from Japan in the 18th century. The common name refers to its planting as a shade tree in the grounds of pagodas and temples. It is usually placed in the genus *Sophora*, but modern research suggests that it should be moved to a new genus, *Styphnolobium*. It is one of the many members of the legume family which have flowers like a pea's. They comprise five petals arranged with two 'keels' at the base, a 'wing' on each side and a 'standard' which acts like an umbrella over the top. Black locust (page 254) also has this type of flower. Pagoda tree needs a hot sunny summer to set the flower buds. In dull or wet summers the floral display is much poorer, while young trees generally do not flower. It is useful as a specimen tree for flowering late in the summer, but has no autumn color.

Sophora japonica makes a domed crown. The green leaves act as a foil for the creamy-white flowers in late summer.

BARK
Dark brown or gray, folded or broadly ridged.

Yellowwood

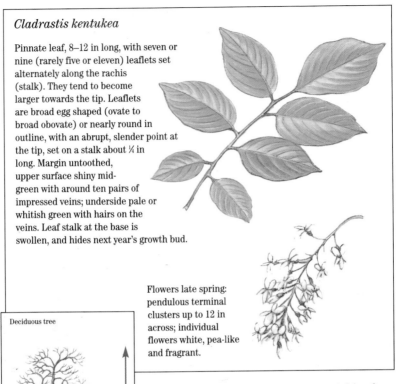

Cladrastis kentukea

Pinnate leaf, 8–12 in long, with seven or nine (rarely five or eleven) leaflets set alternately along the rachis (stalk). They tend to become larger towards the tip. Leaflets are broad egg shaped (ovate to broad obovate) or nearly round in outline, with an abrupt, slender point at the tip, set on a stalk about ¼ in long. Margin untoothed, upper surface shiny mid-green with around ten pairs of impressed veins; underside pale or whitish green with hairs on the veins. Leaf stalk at the base is swollen, and hides next year's growth bud.

Flowers late spring: pendulous terminal clusters up to 12 in across; individual flowers white, pea-like and fragrant.

Deciduous tree

Up to 50 ft

Yellowwood is native to an area stretching from southwestern Virginia, west North Carolina and northeastern Georgia to eastern Oklahoma and then north to southern Indiana. It is seen in scattered stands in hardwood forests, preferring moist sites, and is especially fond of limestone cliffs, streams, or deep mountain valleys. The flowers are fragrant and carried in large clusters in spring. This showy quality explains yellowwood's popularity as a landscape tree across the U.S.A. The fruits are a small legume pod, similar to those of black locust (page 254). Besides *Cladrastis kentukea*, another common scientific name for the tree is *Cladrastis lutea*. When first exposed, the wood is a bright yellow in color, but it darkens to light brown. The genus name is from Greek, and translates as 'brittle branch', referring to the fragility of the twigs and branches. Among trees with pinnate leaves, yellowwood is unusual in that the leaflets are set alternately along the stalk, whereas in most the leaflets are in more or less opposite pairs. The buds are also unusual: they are 'naked', that is, lacking protective bud scales.

Cladrastis kentukea makes a low, spreading tree with a broad rounded crown, often as broad as it is high.

BARK
Both young and mature bark is smooth and gray, similar to beech's.

Kentucky coffee tree

Gymnocladus dioica

Leaf is enormous, up to 36 in by 24 in, set alternately on the shoot, bi- or doubly pinnate, but with no terminal leaflet. Two to four single leaflets at the base, then three to eight pinnate segments with six to fourteen leaflets. Leaflets are egg shaped (ovate), 1–2 ½ in by ⁵⁄₁₆–⅝₆ in, tapering to an acute or short, slender point. Margins untoothed, upper surface matte green, underside glaucous green.

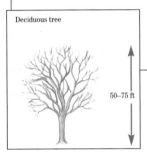

Shoot very stout, pale buff-brown in the first winter with a waxy bloom. Later gray-brown and flaky. Buds flat domed, yellow-brown or dark brown.

In spring, the flowers are carried as large terminal clusters. Individual flowers are greenish white, with four to five spreading petals. They are followed by the dark red-brown pods which are 4–7 in by 1 ½–2 in. These contain six to nine ¾ in ovoid, bony seeds.

Deciduous tree

50–75 ft

Kentucky coffee tree is native to the swath of territory from New York State just into southern Ontario and Minnesota; also south to Oklahoma. It grows on moist river valley sites, where it is a scattered tree with other hardwoods. The leaves have forty or more leaflets and, although these are individually small, together they make a large leaf. While the tree is in leaf during the summer, it appears to be a mass of small leaves; but the large size of the leaves means that the shoots are well spaced. So after the leaves fall, the tree appears rather gaunt, with well-spaced, very stout twigs. The genus name translates as 'naked branch,' and refers to this feature. The tree leafs late in spring and is one of the first to lose its leaves in the fall, when they turn yellow, further exaggerating the gaunt appearance.

The seeds are poisonous when raw, but can be roasted to make a coffee substitute. The timber is reddish-brown, with only a very narrow sapwood layer. It is used in cabinet making.

Gymnocladus dioica has a narrow, open crown with coarse branching off a short trunk.

BARK
Rough, gray and deeply furrowed, with hard, thin scaly ridges. In young trees smooth.

Honey locust

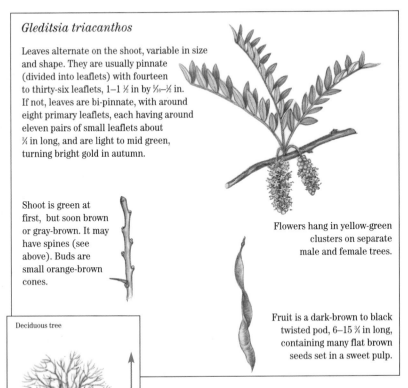

Gleditsia triacanthos

Leaves alternate on the shoot, variable in size and shape. They are usually pinnate (divided into leaflets) with fourteen to thirty-six leaflets, 1–1 ½ in by ⅜–½ in. If not, leaves are bi-pinnate, with around eight primary leaflets, each having around eleven pairs of small leaflets about ¾ in long, and are light to mid green, turning bright gold in autumn.

Shoot is green at first, but soon brown or gray-brown. It may have spines (see above). Buds are small orange-brown cones.

Flowers hang in yellow-green clusters on separate male and female trees.

Fruit is a dark-brown to black twisted pod, 6–15 ¾ in long, containing many flat brown seeds set in a sweet pulp.

Deciduous tree

49–82 ft

Honey locust is native to eastern North America in an area bounded by South Dakota, Ontario to Pennsylvania in the north and northern Florida to southeastern Texas in the south. It is appreciated for the pleasant, light, dappled shade provided by the deeply divided leaves. The tree's wild form is armed with large three-pronged spines, up to 8 in in length. These can be on the shoots, but are also produced directly from the trunk, where they can form large clusters. They are an attractive feature, but very sharp, and can be a safety hazard if honey locusts are planted beside roads. Selective breeding has produced forms without spines, such as var. *inermis,* and these are preferred for ornamental planting. The clone 'Sunburst' is part of var. *inermis*; its new foliage in the spring is golden yellow, maturing to yellow-green. The sweet fleshy pulp surrounding the seeds has a purpose. The pod does not open to release the seeds, but is intended to be eaten by a large mammal. The seed's thick coat is broken down by the animal's stomach acids, and in due course the seed is planted away from the parent tree in the animal's manure.

Gleditsia triacanthos makes a tall tree which usually loses its lower foliage to display the trunk. The leaves turn a fine gold color in autumn.

BARK
Blackish gray or purplish gray and rough, becoming scaly with long narrow ridges on old trees. The bark may have three-pronged spines.

Silver wattle or acacia

Acacia dealbata

In late winter, flowers open into 2 ¾–6 in long heads from buds set the previous year. Fragrant, globe shaped bright yellow flowers ³⁄₁₆–¼ in in diameter.

Bi-pinnate leaves (see honey locust, page 262) 4–6 in by 1 ½–2 ⅓ in, with even numbers of leaflets. The smallest division, 'pinnules' (⅛–⁵⁄₃₂ in), are in about fifty pairs on each of the two dozen or so pairs of larger (1–1 ½ in) leaflets. Leaves are gray-green, with some silky hairs, but new ones are golden brown.

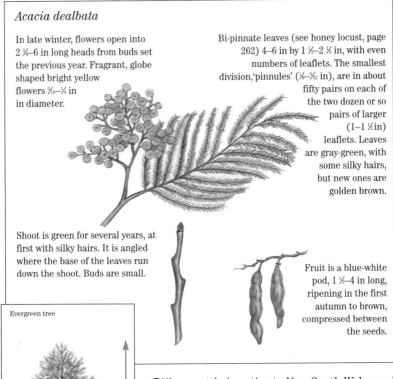

Shoot is green for several years, at first with silky hairs. It is angled where the base of the leaves run down the shoot. Buds are small.

Fruit is a blue-white pod, 1 ½–4 in long, ripening in the first autumn to brown, compressed between the seeds.

Evergreen tree

20–66 ft

Silver wattle is native to New South Wales and Victoria in southeastern mainland Australia; also to Tasmania. It is widely cultivated in mild areas of North America as a winter-flowering tree; likely to be cut back by hard winters, unless killed outright, it usually regrows either from the stump or from root suckers. The flowers are sold by florists who know it, like many people, as 'mimosa'. However, the true mimosa is a different genus and hardy only in mild areas. *Acacia dealbata* belongs to the legume family, and has a typical legume fruit, but in common with *Gleditsia*, it does not have pea-shaped flowers. The attraction of silver wattle flowers are not the petals, but the massed, showy stamens.

Acacia is a large genus, with around 1,200 different species, especially common in Australia and Africa. In Africa, they are typical trees of the savannah. Most *Acacia* species have large spines (fortunately absent in silver wattle) derived from the stipules (see black locust, page 254). Acacias are adapted to regions that have long, dry periods. Many of them cope with lack of water by not having leaves but tough, modified green shoots called phyllodes.

264

Acacia dealbata is flamboyant in
late winter when the bright yellow
flowers dominate the leaves. It
makes a cone or column shaped
tree and has attractive foliage.

BARK
Blue-green and smooth on
young trees, but becoming
corrugated and chocolate-
brown, then gray or black
on old trees.

Silk-tree or mimosa

Albizia julibrissin

Leaves (6–15 in) alternate on the shoot. 'Doubly pinnate'—that is, consisting of five to twelve pairs of primary leaflets, each composed of fifteen to thirty pairs of small, fernlike leaflets (pinnules), ¼–⅜ in long by ¹⁄₁₀–¼ in wide. Pale green, with fine hairs on the underside.

Fruit is a pendulous yellow-brown pod, 5–8 in long, containing several shiny brown seeds.

Flowers at the end of the branches in summer, crowded into ball-like heads with ten or more blooms that have many hairy-silky filaments, rose-pink at the tips.

Deciduous tree

Up to 50 ft

The silk-tree is native to Asia from the Caspian forests in northern Iran and the Caucasus region to the north and from there east into China. It is widely planted (and now naturalized) for its attractive, fernlike foliage and long flowering season. It is seen from Maryland (zone 6) south to Florida and from there west to Texas; it is also in California. It does best on dry, gravelly soils, where, as a legume, it can make its own nitrogen fertilizer. The attraction of the flowers is a product of the massed stamens, which give them a 'powder-puff' appearance. The stamens are silky and slender, an inch in length, and tipped rose-pink, with a small anther. This is one of the many trees called 'mimosa'. The true mimosa is in fact a genus of herbaceous plants whose foliage is sensitive to being touched—the leaves just curl up. In the silk tree, they do not do so, but they do roll up each evening as the light fades. Woman's tongue or *Albizia lebbeck* (originating in tropical Asia) is grown in southern Florida. It has only two to four pairs of primary leaflets, each with three to seven pairs of leaflets, although each is substantially larger, up to 2 in by 1 ¼ in. The flowers are fragrant and greenish white or yellow.

Albizia julibrissin forms a low tree, usually only 30 ft high, but often wider.

BARK
Smooth; gray or gray-brown to black on young and mature barks.

Golden rain tree

Koelreuteria paniculata

Pinnate leaves (divided into leaflets) up to 17 ¾ in. Pink, reddish or yellowish when young. They have five to six pairs of leaflets which are often partially pinnate (in other words, partly bi-pinnate). See honey locust, page 262.

Flowers in August form in large terminal clusters (8–16 in) containing many rich yellow blooms with strap-like petals.

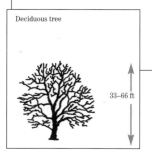

Shoot is coppery brown when young, later light brown. Buds (¼ in) are conical, green and brown.

Leaflets are egg shaped, up to 3 in by 2 in. Margin has large rounded teeth. Upper surface is dark green, underside light green.

Fruit is an inflated papery bladder (1 ½–2 in) with three sections, each with a single black or dark-brown, pea-sized seed.

Deciduous tree

33–66 ft

Golden rain tree is native to China, Japan and Korea. It is also known as Pride of India. It acquired this name at a time when the terms 'India' or 'Indian' were applied to almost anything from the Orient and many things from the west (such as the West Indies and Red Indians). While the flowers can fairly be described as golden, they do not 'rain' but are carried erect above the foliage or spreading out from the ends of the shoots. The name golden rain tree is also used for *Laburnum* which has the attribute of flowers hanging down as if raining. The scientific name commemorates J. Koelreute, an 18th-century naturalist from Karlsba,and the technical shape of the flower clusters, which are in a panicle (a branched or compound raceme). Golden rain tree makes a welcome ornamental tree in central, southern parts of the U.S.A. because it flowers in August, when there are few other trees in bloom. It needs a long, hot summer in order to produce the best floral display and should be sited where it can get the most light. The large leaves turn yellow in autumn, changing from purple-green to brown. The seeds rattle around in the dry papery capsules and are dispersed by the wind.

Koelreuteria paniculata has a rounded crown formed from radiating branches on a short trunk. The large compound leaves cast only a light shade.

BARK
Mature bark is brown or purple-brown; rough, with narrow orange fissures.

Yellow buckeye

Aesculus octandra

The leaves are compound, like a palm's, and in opposite pairs, with five stalked egg shaped (obovate) to elliptic leaflets. These are 4–8 in by 1 ½–3 in and taper to a slender, tail-like tip. Margin has regular, rounded-pointed teeth. Upper surface is deep green with fifteen to twenty pairs of veins. Underside whitish green or yellow-green, and often hairy.

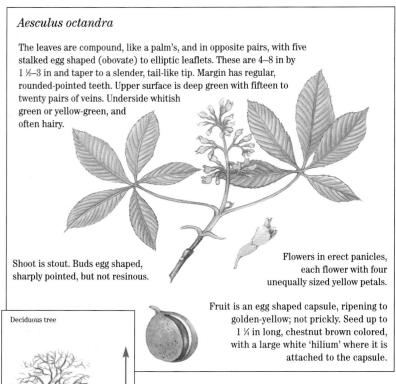

Shoot is stout. Buds egg shaped, sharply pointed, but not resinous.

Flowers in erect panicles, each flower with four unequally sized yellow petals.

Fruit is an egg shaped capsule, ripening to golden-yellow; not prickly. Seed up to 1 ¼ in long, chestnut brown colored, with a large white 'hilium' where it is attached to the capsule.

Deciduous tree

60–90 ft

Yellow buckeye is native from Pennsylvania south to Alabama and Georgia and west just into southern Illinois, and is especially numerous in the Great Smoky Mountains National Park. Found on moist sites, or on rich, deep hillsides, it is a component of mixed forests. This is the tallest and largest of the American species of *Aesculus*. The common name, buckeye, refers to the pale patch or 'hilium' on the seed, where the developing seed is attached to the placenta—like the human navel. The seeds are poisonous, but early Native Americans roasted and soaked them to remove the toxic element.

Ohio buckeye, *Aesculus glabra*, has a wider distribution than yellow buckeye, extending farther west into Oklahoma and Iowa. It makes a smaller tree, usually less than 50 feet high. The easiest way to identify it is by the leaves, which have seven leaflets, and the fruit, which is rough, with triangular pimples or warts. The bark has a fetid smell. Red buckeye, *Aesculus pavia*, is smaller still, usually no more than 25 ft high.The flowers are bright red, rarely yellow-red.

Aesculus octandra has a broad, rounded or domed crown.

BARK
Gray to brown, fissuring into large scaly plates.

Horse chestnut

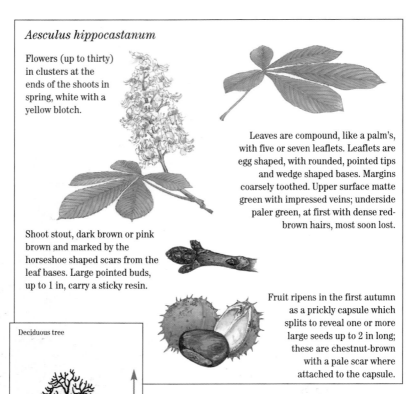

Aesculus hippocastanum

Flowers (up to thirty) in clusters at the ends of the shoots in spring, white with a yellow blotch.

Leaves are compound, like a palm's, with five or seven leaflets. Leaflets are egg shaped, with rounded, pointed tips and wedge shaped bases. Margins coarsely toothed. Upper surface matte green with impressed veins; underside paler green, at first with dense red-brown hairs, most soon lost.

Shoot stout, dark brown or pink brown and marked by the horseshoe shaped scars from the leaf bases. Large pointed buds, up to 1 in, carry a sticky resin.

Deciduous tree

66–115 ft

Fruit ripens in the first autumn as a prickly capsule which splits to reveal one or more large seeds up to 2 in long; these are chestnut-brown with a pale scar where attached to the capsule.

Horse chestnut is native to a small area of northern Greece and southern Albania where it has survived since the most recent ice age. (When it was first introduced to Europe in the 1500s it was believed to come from Turkey.) It quickly established itself as part of our tree heritage and is widely planted for its flowers and as an ornamental or shade tree. The name refers to the fruits or nuts, which can be fed in small quantities to animals. To humans they are bitter—and inedible—but have had a limited use in perfume manufacture.

Horse chestnut does everything in a rush in the spring—like daffodils. Adult trees rarely produce a second flush of foliage; if the first set is lost, the tree normally waits until the next spring before making any new ones. Branches with the large sticky buds make a pleasant winter decoration if stood in a vase. The wood is soft, easily split and of no real quality. Pink horse chestnut (*Aesculus carnea*) is a hybrid with red buckeye and horse chestnut, with darker leaves and pink or red flowers.

Aesculus hippocastanum has a
tall, domed crown. In spring it is
clothed by the large erect candles
of flowers. The foliage may turn
scarlet, gold, orange or a pale,
dull brown in autumn.

BARK
Red-brown or gray-brown,
smooth on young trees
but developing thick scale;
on old trees it is fissured
at the base.

California palm

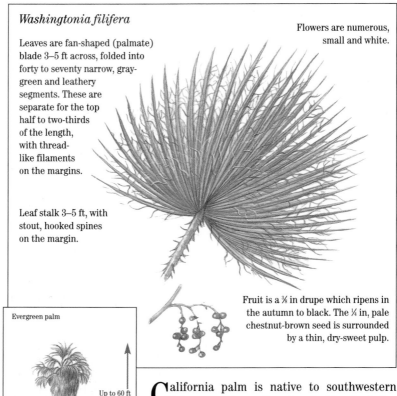

Washingtonia filifera

Flowers are numerous, small and white.

Leaves are fan-shaped (palmate) blade 3–5 ft across, folded into forty to seventy narrow, gray-green and leathery segments. These are separate for the top half to two-thirds of the length, with thread-like filaments on the margins.

Leaf stalk 3–5 ft, with stout, hooked spines on the margin.

Fruit is a ⅜ in drupe which ripens in the autumn to black. The ¼ in, pale chestnut-brown seed is surrounded by a thin, dry-sweet pulp.

Evergreen palm

Up to 60 ft

California palm is native to southwestern Arizona and to southeastern California; it also occurs in northern Baja California, Mexico. In the wild it is found on moist soils, especially alkaline ones, beside rivers or in canyon bottoms. It is widely cultivated outside this native area.

The palm's habit is monopodal, meaning literally 'one foot'. That is, the stem is unbranched, with all the growth being made from the bud at the top of the stem. The new leaves are erect, but turn horizontal as they mature and eventually hang down dead, something like a petticoat, giving the tree its alternate name, 'petticoat palm'. The flowers are carried on clusters up to 10 ft in length, which emerge in the axils of younger leaves. The fruits have an edible layer and were collected by Native Americans, either to be eaten fresh or dried and stored. The seeds were pounded into meal or flour.

California palm's close relative, Mexican *Washingtonia* (*Washingtonia robusta*) is found in Baja California but is also cultivated in southern California and along the Gulf Coast to Florida.

Washingtonia filifera makes a
single-stemmed tree with all
the foliage at the top. The dead
leaves hang down like a petticoat
in mature trees.

BARK
Smooth and reddish
brown, with horizontal
lines from the bases of
fallen leaves.

Chinese fan palm

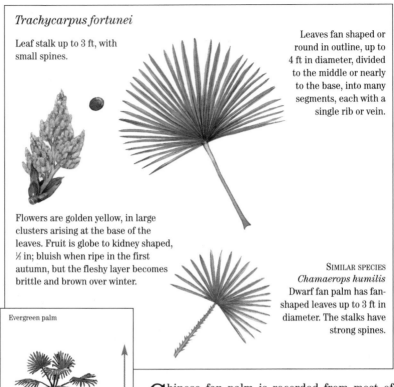

Trachycarpus fortunei

Leaf stalk up to 3 ft, with small spines.

Leaves fan shaped or round in outline, up to 4 ft in diameter, divided to the middle or nearly to the base, into many segments, each with a single rib or vein.

Flowers are golden yellow, in large clusters arising at the base of the leaves. Fruit is globe to kidney shaped, ½ in; bluish when ripe in the first autumn, but the fleshy layer becomes brittle and brown over winter.

SIMILAR SPECIES
Chamaerops humilis
Dwarf fan palm has fan-shaped leaves up to 3 ft in diameter. The stalks have strong spines.

Evergreen palm

Up to 49 ft

Chinese fan palm is recorded from most of southern China south into northern Vietnam and northern Burma, but is unlikely to be native throughout this area. Man has been planting it for many centuries for its fiber, which is produced at the base of the leaves, wraps the trunk in a protective layer, and can be removed in small sheets—a natural unwoven cloth. The Yi minority peoples in Yunnan use it to make rainwear, wearing the sheets over the back so that they shed rain much like a thatched roof. The leaf fibers are also used for weaving. Though the hardiest of the palms, it is tender as a young plant. It is hardy south of a line from central North Carolina to central Texas and on the West Coast.

Dwarf fan palm or European fan palm is native to the western Mediterranean region, where it is common in dry evergreen scrub along the western coast of Italy, southern Spain and North Africa. In the US, it is hardy in mild areas. It only rarely makes a tree but can grow up to 20–30 ft in cultivation. The species is very similar to *Trachycarpus fortunei*, but easily separated by its shrub-like shape, with its several unbranched stems, and the prominent spines on the leaf stalk.

Trachycarpus fortunei has only a
single stem, with the leaves
restricted to a tuft at the top,
where live leaves spread upwards
and outwards and the older dead
leaves hang down.

BARK
Covered by the fibrous red-
brown to dull brown bases
of the leaves
(see photograph), but
where removed it is gray,
with ridges made by the
fallen leaves.

Canary Island palm

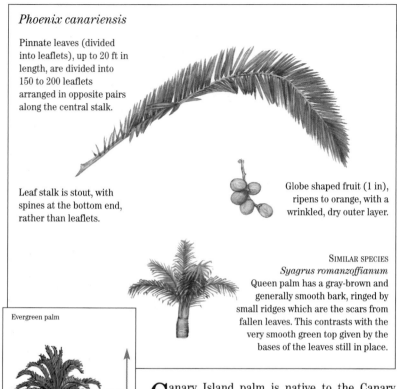

Phoenix canariensis

Pinnate leaves (divided into leaflets), up to 20 ft in length, are divided into 150 to 200 leaflets arranged in opposite pairs along the central stalk.

Leaf stalk is stout, with spines at the bottom end, rather than leaflets.

Globe shaped fruit (1 in), ripens to orange, with a wrinkled, dry outer layer.

SIMILAR SPECIES
Syagrus romanzoffianum
Queen palm has a gray-brown and generally smooth bark, ringed by small ridges which are the scars from fallen leaves. This contrasts with the very smooth green top given by the bases of the leaves still in place.

Evergreen palm

49–66 ft

Canary Island palm is native to the Canary Islands and widely planted in warmer parts of the U.S.A. as an ornamental tree. It can make majestic specimens, with trunks up to 3 ft in diameter. It is allied to the date palm (page 280), but does not sucker, so it is a neater tree for ornamental use. However, the fruit is not edible.

Palms belong to the large group of plants known as monocots, a name derived from the term monocotyledon, which describes the single cotyledon or seed leaf produced by the germinating seed. Grasses, bamboos, orchids and bulbs such as daffodils are all monocots. A characteristic of monocots is their inability to make secondary thickening of the trunk. The full diameter has to be made as it grows: it cannot be increased, as in other trees, by later laying down new wood and bark. If a palm tree goes through a lean period, the trunk formed at this time may be thinner than the trunk above.

Queen palm is native to Brazil and Argentina and planted in mild areas as a shapely ornamental. It is sometimes put in a genus of its own as *Arecastrum romanzoffianum*.

Phoenix canariensis makes a striking ornamental tree with its long, finely divided leaves and stout bole.

BARK
Initially hidden by the fibrous leaf bases, but when these fall it looks gray and rough because of the leaf-base scars.

Date palm

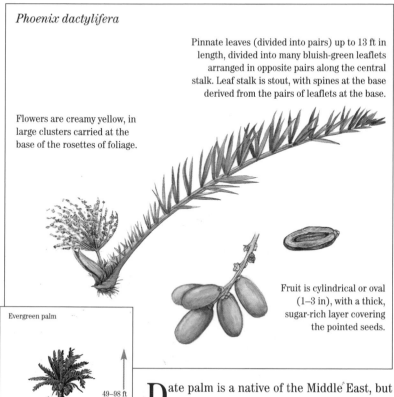

Phoenix dactylifera

Pinnate leaves (divided into pairs) up to 13 ft in length, divided into many bluish-green leaflets arranged in opposite pairs along the central stalk. Leaf stalk is stout, with spines at the base derived from the pairs of leaflets at the base.

Flowers are creamy yellow, in large clusters carried at the base of the rosettes of foliage.

Fruit is cylindrical or oval (1–3 in), with a thick, sugar-rich layer covering the pointed seeds.

Evergreen palm

49–98 ft

Date palm is a native of the Middle East, but has been cultivated for so many centuries that it is impossible to work out its natural distribution. It thrives in hot, dry regions provided it has access to moisture at the roots. Its fruit—the dates—are delicious when raw and are a staple food for many millions of people. They are easily dried when the sugar content rises to 50 percent, allowing them to be kept for long periods. Date palm leaves are used for thatching and weaving; the trunk provides timber; and freshly felled trees ooze a sweet sap which can be fermented to make an alcoholic drink.

Date plum is widely planted as an ornamental tree in southern Florida and there are commercial fruit plantations in southeastern California. As an ornamental tree it lacks the grace and poise of the related Canary Island palm (page 278), having a much more slender trunk, rarely more than 1 ft in diameter. It also produces suckers around the base of the trunk. These provide an alternate means of propagation, but are inconvenient in specimen trees planted beside boulevards.

Phoenix dactylifera makes a slender-trunked tree surrounded by suckers at the base.

BARK
Initially the fibrous leaf bases cover the trunk, but these fall to reveal the true bark as gray and rough—a result of scars left by fallen leaves.

Joshua tree

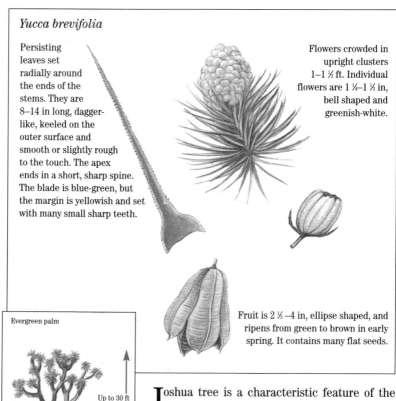

Yucca brevifolia

Persisting leaves set radially around the ends of the stems. They are 8–14 in long, dagger-like, keeled on the outer surface and smooth or slightly rough to the touch. The apex ends in a short, sharp spine. The blade is blue-green, but the margin is yellowish and set with many small sharp teeth.

Flowers crowded in upright clusters 1–1 ½ ft. Individual flowers are 1 ¼–1 ½ in, bell shaped and greenish-white.

Fruit is 2 ½ –4 in, ellipse shaped, and ripens from green to brown in early spring. It contains many flat seeds.

Evergreen palm

Up to 30 ft

Joshua tree is a characteristic feature of the Mohave Desert from southern Nevada, western Arizona, and southeastern California just into the southwestern corner of Utah. It occurs on dry soils, from the plains at the bottom, the slopes on the sides, and the tops of mesas. Flowers occur at the ends of the branches and further growth is made from lateral buds causing the branch to fork. The forking of a branch shows how many times the tree has flowered. The tree was given its name by early Mormons, who considered that the habit resembled Joshua's arms as he led the Israelites into the Promised Land. The tree is important for wildlife, with birds using holes bored into the branches for nest sites. Small mammals use the leaves for food and bedding, and lizards rest during the day among the old dead leaves. The fruit is a capsule, but instead of breaking open on the tree to scatter the seeds, it falls intact to the ground. The seeds can be ground into a meal, and the roots provide a red dye. Six other species of *Yucca* can be tree-sized and are found across the southernmost states along the Gulf Coast and up the southeastern coastal plain. All have longer leaves than the Joshua tree.

Yucca brevifolia makes a gaunt specimen, with its ascending-spreading branches with tufts of foliage towards the tips and dead leaves behind.

BARK

Gray or brown, and rough from the fallen leaves. It becomes corky and deeply fissured into plates.

Index of common and Latin names

Similar species are listed under the principal spreads (e.g., *Cerasus avium*, see *Prunus avium* **180**).

Specialist guides covering the full range of North American trees:

Audubon Society Field Guide to North American Trees, Eastern region and Western region, Elbert Little, Knopf.

Checklist of United States Trees, USDA Handbook 541

Flora of North America, Oxford University Press, New York